D0197074

MICMAC
BY CHOICE
Elsie Sark – an Island legend

M. Olga McKenna

Formac Publishing Company Limited
Halifax, 1990

Canadian Cataloguing in Publication Data

McKenna, Mary Olga, 1920-

Micmac by Choice: Elsie Sark-an island legend
  ISBN 0-88780-077-7

  1. Sark, Elsie. 2. Lennox Island (P.E.I.) —
  Biography. 3. Micmac Indians — Biography. 4. Indians of North America — Prince Edward Island. I. Title.
FC2649.L56Z49 1990   971.7"1 C90-097607-1
F1049.5.L56M35 1990

Cover photo: Elsie Maud Houghton, 1918
(Courtesy Holborn Library, London)

Formac Publishing Company Limited
5502 Atlantic Street
Halifax, Nova Scotia
B3H 1G4

Printed and bound in Canada

5 4 3 2 1 90 91 92 93 94

Contents

To my maternal grandmother,
Rose Askin Monaghan (1866-1948),
one of the unsung "women worthies" of
Prince Edward Island.

Acknowledgements

In the almost total absence of written material of an autobiographical or personal nature relating to Elsie Houghton Sark, the writer found it necessary to engage in a variety of data gathering activities in Canada and the United Kingdom. These included visiting the places where she had lived and worked; ferreting out extant records (public and private), registers, newspapers, letters, tapes, written articles; and, interviewing those who knew her personally or by hearsay, particularly her family, relatives, friends, neighbours, teachers, doctors, nurses, politicians, religious and clergy. Fortunately there were no research barriers and the writer is indebted to sources too numerous to document individually.

My thanks go, first of all, to my religious congregation, the Sisters of Charity, Halifax, who have given me the support necessary to bring the project through to completion; to Mrs. Hesta MacDonald who, when Public Relations Officer at Holland College, suggested the project in the first place and encouraged me to undertake it; to the Prince Edward Island Women's History Project, a dedicated volunteer group, who sponsored the work; to Mount Saint Vincent University and the Prince Edward Island Office of the Secretary of State for their financial assistance.

The Houghton-Sark families have been most generous with their time and knowledge. I am grateful to each of the Sark children who were most co-operative from the beginning to the end of the study. Through quiet conversations with Mrs. Sark's three daughters— Sister Martha, CND; Sister Rebecca, CSM; and the late Mrs. Joan Beaudin—the writer gained invaluable insight into Elsie Sark as mother and counsellor. Her three sons and their wives—Raymond and Frances, Jack and Marilyn, Charles and Doreen—were particularly helpful in providing names of relatives and friends, in making available family records and artifacts, and being supportive in every way they could. Special mention must be made of Mrs. Sark's sister, Ellen (Nellie) Rebecca Houghton Taylor, the sole surviving member of the Houghton family, and her husband, Wilfred, a veteran of World War I, who not only welcomed the writer to their home in Totton, Southampton, on four different visits to England, but also made available pertinent documents, photographs and other memorabilia in their possession. In her 84th year, Nellie accompanied the writer to Dover and literally retraced on foot all the places of significance in her sister's life prior to her emigration to Canada. Wilfred (Will) Taylor, in his 90th year, drove the writer to all the places in Southhampton visited by his sister-in-law on the occasion of her visits to England in 1949 and 1964.

To the many people who provided information through oral interviews, my sincere thanks. Often a casual word or phrase opened up new avenues of research which resulted in priceless nuggets of information. Noteworthy among those interviewed were Micmac Indians of the Lennox Island Band; Micmac Indians of the Abegweit Band; Mrs. Sark's nieces, Mrs. Sarah Tuplin, wife of the late Joe Tuplin and Mrs. Eleanor Callow; her nephews, James Sark, present Chief of the Abegweit Band; Cyrus Sark, and John Joe Sark; residents of the Port Hill, Tyne Valley and Grand River communities, especially Mrs. Bessie MacNeil, Mrs. Jessie Brown and Mrs. Beatrice MacKinnon and Mrs. Marguerite Maynard; Mrs. Mina Strongman of St. Eleanor's; Dr. Catherine Hennessey and Ms. Clare McQuade of Charlottetown; Mrs. Doris Murphy of Summerside; my good friend Jane Archibald of Indian Harbour, Nova Scotia, herself a World War II bride from England. Without the assistance of these and the more than one hundred interviewees, this work would not have been possible.

Librarians, archivists and their assistants in the United Kingdom and in Canada were consistently helpful. To the following, my special thanks: The P.E.I. Heritage Foundation; the Public Archives (P.E.I.); the Robertson Library, (U.P.E.I.); the National Library of Canada (Ottawa); the Public Archives of Canada (Ottawa); the Federal Department of Indian and Inuit Affairs (Amherst, N.S.): the British Library (London); the Public Record Offices (London); the Holborn Library (London); the Hanwell Hospital (London); the Ealing Public Library (London); and the Library of Congress (Washington, D.C.).

And, finally, the writer is most grateful for the many services provided in the preparation of the manuscript by Mrs. Peggy Stephens and her efficient secretarial staff at Mount Saint Vincent University and Mrs. Mary Lou Brousseau, Secretariat, Mount Saint Vincent Motherhouse; for the helpful comments of those who reviewed the initial draft: Dr. Margaret Conrad of Acadia University,

ACKNOWLEDGEMENTS

Dr. Harold McGee of Saint Mary's University, Dr. Andrew Robb of the University of Prince Edward Island, and Mrs. Doreen Sark, Principal of the Lennox Island Day School; for Ms. Elizabeth Eve's perceptive editorial improvements in the final manuscript; and the countless contributions of family and friends on Prince Edward Island whose consistent interest in the project has been a powerful source of strength and inspiration throughout.

Mary Olga McKenna, SC, Professor Emeritus
Mount Saint Vincent University

Introduction

In April 1973, as Elsie Maud Houghton Sark made her first and last journey by car across the newly-constructed causeway connecting the Lennox Island Indian Reserve with the mainland of Prince Edward Island, she asked the driver to stop midway while she offered a prayer of thanksgiving to God. From the time this woman from England arrived on the Reserve in 1918 as wife of John J. Sark, soldier son of the Micmac Indian Chief, she strove relentlessly to overcome the isolation of the Micmac community on the Lennox Island Reserve. The long-awaited causeway provided a means of access which promised a new era for the Reserve.

Mrs. John Sark's life story ranks among the unwritten legends of Prince Edward Island. Her virtues have been extolled by three generations of non-Indian Islanders. From their perspective, the material causeway, officially opened three months after her death, was symbolic of the cultural bridge she had helped to construct between the Micmac Indians on the Reserve and the white communities on the mainland of Prince Edward Island, throughout the fifty-five years of her tenure there.

When growing up on Prince Edward Island in the 1930s, I had often heard of the legendary Mrs. John Sark. I understood that she was a nurse from England who married a Micmac soldier during the First World War, that she came to Canada after the war, settled with her husband on Lennox Island and dedicated her life to the betterment of the Indians; she was their Florence Nightingale. When, therefore, I was asked to make a contribution to Island

Women's Studies, the name that came to mind was Mrs. John Sark. This choice was received enthusiastically. In 1981 the Zonta Club of Charlottetown had paid tribute to her as one of the outstanding women of Prince Edward Island. One of her long-time associates succinctly summarized the high regard in which she is still held, almost two decades after her death: "I have known many estimable women in my long life," said octogenarian Sister Mary Henry Mulligan, CSM, LL D, "but never one for whom I had more esteem and awe than Elsie Sark for the work she accomplished among the Indians ... cheerfully and with great inherent grace."

I had never met Mrs. Sark personally and I learned early on that there were no autobiographical materials—no letters, no diaries. Two of her children—the oldest daughter Martha and the youngest son Charlie—informed me their mother was adamant in her refusal to record her life experiences. Mrs. Doris Murphy, a close friend of the Sark family and a would-be biographer, recalled that Mrs. Sark was both fascinated and amused by the fact that anyone would want to write her life story. To reconstruct the story of her life, therefore, it was necessary to travel and search for material in manifold places. I caught glimpses of her as a child, teenager, and young woman from photographs in the possession of her sister in England; as wife, mother, and widow, from prints made available by family and friends in Canada. I heard her voice, and learned snippets of her life from an interview taped by Mrs. Helen Mac-Donald for a CFCY Radio Programme in 1961. I read encomiums of her work and achievements among the Indians in the local newspapers. To get to know her as a real person, however, I was totally dependent on the people who had lived with her, worked with her, known her personally or by hearsay.

After approximately three years of casual conversations and organized interviews with her contemporaries living across the strait from Lennox Island, I was satisfied that I had indeed found the woman for whom I was looking. Mrs. Sark, they assured me, was a grand English lady, a courageous and compassionate woman, a person to be admired for sacrificing a life of ease and comfort in order to enhance the life-style of her husband's people. In the face of almost insurmountable obstacles—isolation, lack of the basic means of communication and physical amenities—she found herself working among the poorest of the economically poor on Prince Edward Island. In their estimation, she was a real saint!

A few months later, however, when I was able to break through the silence of the Micmac community, this image was almost totally shattered. For many of the Indians, Mrs. Sark was a domineering white woman, resented for challenging their native life-style and for abetting the efforts of the federal government to deprive them of their aboriginal culture. Some questioned why I was focusing on the late Mrs. John Sark, the *English* woman, mother of the Chief of the Lennox Island Band. "Why not focus on the late Mrs. Jacob Sark/Mitchell the *French* Acadian wife of John's brother, mother of the Chief of the Abegweit Band?" they asked. Or, more importantly, "Why not one of the *Micmac* women whose contributions to the social and cultural history of the community are little known outside the Reserve?" It was clear from these comments that Elsie Sark was a far more complex and controversial woman than I had anticipated.

Her life fell neatly into three chronological periods, each of which spanned a quarter of a century. Part One of this book focuses on the period from 1892 to 1918, in the context of her family and friends in England; Part Two concentrates on the period from 1918 to 1945 when she came to the Reserve and carried out a wide spectrum of roles—wife, mother, farmer, nurse, post-mistress, social worker, hostess. Part Three centres on the period from 1945 to 1973 and highlights her relationships with her own family and friends during her widowhood.

Here was an English woman, reared with the traditions of the Victorian era. As a young lady, she was not afraid to make decisions about her life, and to take advantage of the emerging status of women. When the first intimation of romantic love came her way in the person of Bombardier John James Sark of the Canadian Expeditionary Forces Overseas, she had no problem making three major breaks with her past— her family, religion, and nationality. The self-reliant, adventurous twenty-four-year-old Elsie Maud Houghton brooked no opposition from family or tradition in her decision to marry the man she loved, even though he was Micmac and Roman Catholic.

When this tall, attractive woman with an easy charm, tranquil demeanour, and sophisticated sense of dress arrived on Lennox Island, she projected the image of an aristocratic lady. Her abrupt manner, her stately bearing, her dry sense of humour, and her outspokenness had initially a disarming effect on the natives. Her personality, her attitudes, and her values were in sharp contrast to theirs. The Protestant work-ethic, for example, so deeply engrained in every fibre of her being from birth, was a far cry from the easy-going life-style of the Micmac ethos.

To understand and appreciate the young Mrs. Sark, whose experiences during this period were so inextricably intertwined with those of the native people, a history of the Lennox Island Band of Micmac Indians became a *sine qua non*.

My personal knowledge of Indians on Prince Edward Island was limited to a small settlement in a place called Indian River, on the outskirts of Kensington, my home town. In the 1930s a few families lived there in wigwams along the river bank in a small wooded area. They were a quiet, shy, and withdrawn people, presumably attempting to live their traditional mode of life insofar as that was possible. They seemed to have a carefree, hand-to-mouth existence. The women and children sold mayflowers in the spring, blueberries in the summer, and potato baskets in the fall; the men hunted, trapped, and fished. This group, I learned, was not representative of the members of the tribe who settled on Reserve land and engaged in farming.

In 1918 there were four small Reserves set aside on Prince Edward Island for the Indians, the majority of whom lived on Lennox Island, the most isolated location. At the time, a government-sponsored agricultural program was in place. Those who participated in it were relatively self-sufficient; conscientious objectors were, of necessity, dependent on welfare. Accordingly, when the Indian Agent, long-time friend and counsellor to John Sark, encouraged John and Elsie to remain on the Reserve, she acquiesced in a typically British manner of whole-hearted resignation, commitment, and dedication. This well-intentioned decision was to put her in the anomalous position of being both an object of admiration and resentment. For one faction, she was a leading spirit in the community; for the other, she was the prototype of white superiority.

Involvement in the Canadian Indian programs paid off for the Sark family. Their farm was the envy of the community during the Depression. A decade later the children were pursuing educational and life careers; by the 1950s, all had left the Reserve, and were seemingly assimilated into the larger Canadian mosaic.

As the legendary figure of the romantic war-bride gradually gave way to the indomitable Mrs. Sark, a Victorian heroine emerged. When Elsie Houghton Sark left Dover and crossed the Atlantic from Liverpool to Lennox Island, she did not leave her values behind nor did she surrender her life ambitions; she continued to live by the Victorian ethic. It was only in the 1960s, when she realized her own pilgrim status, that she was forced to accept the fact that she was the mother of Indian children. Unfolding against a backdrop of inter-racial and cross-cultural tensions, her life story obviously had great potential to shed light on Indian-white relations in Prince Edward Island during the second and third quarters of the twentieth century. Lennox Island, because of its small size and geographic isolation, served as an ideal social laboratory in which the impact of one woman on the social and cultural history of a region could be studied. The project needed no further justification.

Anthropologist Ruth Benedict wrote in an unpublished notebook:

> ...one adventure through the life of one woman who has been profoundly stirred by a great restlessness and you will comprehend more than from a library of theorizing.

Such was my experience. It is this personally exciting and enriching adventure that I want to share with my readers.

M. Olga McKenna, SC
Professor of Emeritus
Mount Saint Vincent University
Halifax, Nova Scotia

Part One
1892 - 1918

There is a tide in the affairs of men,
Which, taken at the flood leads on to victory;
Omitted, all the voyage of their life
Is bound in shallows and in miseries.

Julius Caesar, IV, 3, 217

1 | The Canadian Visitor

As the twenty-three-year-old Elsie Houghton returned to Hanwell Hospital in London, after her leave at home, in Dover, she could hardly contain herself. It was a beautiful April evening and she had no fear of the consequences if she failed to meet the 10 p.m. curfew. There would be the usual verbal rebuke from the porter on desk duty at the nurses' residence and the default would be meticulously recorded in the day book. This did not disturb her. Her one thought was to find her Irish friend, Nurse Margaret Dunne, and share with her the romantic event of the day. She had met a tall, dark, handsome Canadian soldier and had fallen in love with him.

Elsie's brother Harry, who was stationed with the Twenty-fourth Battery of the Canadian Expeditionary Force at nearby Shorncliffe Camp, invited a comrade-in-arms, Bombardier John J. Sark, to his home in Dover for Sunday dinner. Doubtless entranced by the beauty of the young lady seated across the table from him, this naturally reticent Micmac Indian was encouraged to tell stories about his own family background and his reasons for enlisting in the army. His audience—the Houghton family—learned early-on that their guest was not the typical Canadian non-commissioned officer.

For Elsie, John's personal history must have unfolded like a fairy tale. He was the son of John Thomas Sark, Chief of the Micmac Indians on Prince Edward Island; his mother, Margaret Thornton Sark, had died five years before, in 1910. Both parents were native Islanders but came from opposite ends of the province—his father from Malpeque in Prince County, his mother from Montague in Kings County. He himself was born in the United States because at the time of his birth, November 2, 1888, the Sark family were settled temporarily in Houlton, Maine, along with other migrant Micmac families.

When John was just three days old, he was taken across the nearby Canadian border to Debec in Carleton County, New Brunswick, to be baptized in the Roman Catholic church of St. Agnes. While he was still an infant, the family moved back to Prince Edward Island and settled on Lennox Island, located in Richmond Bay (later known as Malpeque Bay), approximately one mile off the northwest coast. It was here on October 22, 1900, at the age of twelve, he was confirmed in the Roman Catholic faith by the bishop of the Charlottetown diocese, Bishop J.C. McDonald. It was here, too, in the one-room schoolhouse, under the tutelage of Casimir Poirier and John F. Arsenault, he successfully completed the program of studies of the provincial schools. At the age of seventeen he was admitted to Saint Dunstan's, a Roman Catholic college in Charlottetown.

During his years there (1905-1909), besides being academically successful, John Sark earned the social distinction of being the greatest rugby player in the province. His colleagues were reputed to have said of him, "When in action he moved with the velocity of a hurricane and no man, red or white, could withstand the shock of his two hundred and ten pounds."[1]

After graduating in 1909, he applied to the Prince Edward Island Board of Education for a public-school teaching license and on July 23 was granted a third-class teaching certificate. For the next five years he taught in the federally-supported Indian day school on the Lennox Island Reserve.

When John Sark was convinced that England had good reason to be at war, he responded to the second call to the colours in the fall of 1914. He was eager to be part of the effort to uphold the principles for which England as a nation stood. Accordingly, he resigned from his temporary job with the Intercolonial Railway (I.C.R.) in New Brunswick and went to Fredericton to enlist. He was assigned to the Twenty-fourth Battery of the Canadian Overseas Expeditionary Force as a non-commissioned officer with the rank of bombardier.

He was among the fortunate half of the battery which was granted leave at Christmas; the scheduled February leaves were cancelled. It was his first and last visit home in uniform prior to his overseas assignment. On February 18, following Mass at the Roman Catholic Church of Saint Dunstan, and for Anglicans, communion services at Christ Church, and after receiving Bibles from the Canadian Branch of the British and Foreign Bible Society, the Twenty-third and Twenty-fourth Batteries were given a rousing send-off by the many patriotic individuals and groups in Fredericton. There was more fanfare en route to, and in Halifax.[2] Their fellow Canadians were proud of them.

The trip across the Atlantic was, of course, veiled in secrecy because of the German blockade of the British Isles, and excitement was aroused when a spy was seized from among the civilians aboard the SS *Megantic*, the steamer to which John Sark was assigned. After detouring to Queenstown, on the coast of Ireland, they reached Liverpool on Saturday, March 6. The batteries disembarked at once and went directly to Shorncliffe. They arrived eight hours later and walked to Moore Barracks, about a mile from the railway station. Here, they were to be trained for overseas assignment. On Sundays, they were permitted to go to Folkestone where they took advantage of the public baths and the hospitality of the people. John was grateful for the invitation to Dover. Years later he described his first encounter with Elsie Houghton: "To fall in love with her was my lot, nor did I attempt to conceal my honest affection, which she reciprocated."[3]

Life at the hospital was somehow different for Elsie as she went about her chores in the days and weeks after their meeting. Eventually a postcard arrived addressed to her at the Hanwell Mental Hospital. On one side of the card was a photograph of the Prince Edward Island artillerymen of the Twenty-fourth Battery; second from the right, the handsome John. Quickly, she read the brief message on the reverse side. "In the event anything happens to me, please send this card to my father, Lennox Island, Prince Edward Island. Your Chum." It was evident that either he was on his way or would soon be on his way to the war zone ... and he was interested in her.

Elsie eagerly looked forward to her next two days off duty, when she would learn from her brother the actual state of affairs. Her hunch was confirmed. The Sixth Brigade, on arrival in England, was immediately turned into the Canadian Reserve Battery and the identity of the brigade and batteries disappeared. The personnel were to be used in various Canadian battalions at the front, to replace the already depleted lines. Some members of the Twenty-third and Twenty-fourth Batteries were on the firing lines less than one month after their arrival in England. On March 26, Captain A.T. McKay of Montague, Prince Edward Island, left Shorncliffe with another group for the firing lines in northern France. Approximately two hundred more artillerymen of the same batteries, including Bombardier John Sark, were notified that they were being prepared for immediate action in the field. It was well known that the system of training the Canadians for the front was particularly severe, night and day, without break, under all kinds of weather conditions.

In point of fact, John Sark was not drafted to France until May 28, 1915, but the knowledge that his going to the front was imminent precipitated the development of a close relationship between Elsie and John.[4] They saw each other as often as possible in the time at their disposal. Furthermore, John had no difficulty obtaining the necessary permit to enter the heavily-fortified town of Dover because the Houghtons were a well-respected military family.

During the two-months that they were getting to know each other, they undoubtedly exchanged stories, shared their hopes and their dreams and talked of the future. Before John left for the front lines in France, their friendship had developed to the extent that Elsie risked losing her job at the hospital, by staying away without leave, to be with him for the week preceding his departure.

The relationship was equally serious on John's part; before joining the Canadian Artillery's Third Brigade and crossing the English Channel on June 6, he arranged to have his salary made payable to Elsie. They seem to have decided on a future together, and whether they knew it or not, it would be one which would necessitate Elsie giving up her homeland, her nationality and her religion to be at his side.

At this time of her life, Elsie probably did not count the cost of a future away from her family and indeed may have been looking for a new life. She may have considered following the footsteps of her older brothers, perhaps, in Canada.

The Houghton family into which Elsie was born had its roots firmly fixed in Victorian England. Her father Charles Fisher Houghton came from Shakespeare's birthplace—Stratford-on-Avon. He was orphaned at an early age, and received little, if any, formal education. As a youth, he was employed as a groom, presumably in the household of his guardians. Inspired by the Victorian vision of imperial Britain, he made his way to the Tower of London where, on July 4, 1871, at the age of seventeen, he enlisted in the Royal Artillery. Two days later, he was attested for the Royal Regiment of Artillery in the Thames Police Court and assigned to the Third Brigade. Subsequently he served with the Eleventh Brigade and the London Division which later became the Seventh Eastern Division.

Elsie's mother, Martha Ellis Houghton, came from Ringmer, Sussex. The youngest daughter of Reuben and Rebecca Ellis, she was born on September 13, 1857. Reuben Ellis was an agricultural labourer so Martha, like her older sisters Fanny, Jane and Abigail and her young brother James, attended the local school for children of working-class families. When Gunner Charles F. Houghton was approaching his mid-twenties, he was stationed with the Eleventh Brigade of the Royal Artillery Garrison at Shoeburyness, Essex. There, he met Martha Ellis who was employed as a domestic servant in the area. On April 7, 1880, they were married in the registry office in Rochford, Essex.

Martha Houghton knew well what was expected of her as a woman in the England of her day. As the wife of a soldier, it was her duty to do everything possible to support her husband's career and to develop in their children the virtues of obedience and loyalty to their parents, the Church of England, and the Crown. This she did in true Victorian style. She cheerfully accepted the hardships, frustrations, and inconveniences associated with life in the army and taught her children to work hard, to fear God, and to make themselves useful to society. During the fifteen-year period prior to her husband's retirement from the Royal Artillery, she gave birth to five children, each in a different location. Charles James was born in Shoeburyness in 1881; May, in Gosport in 1884; Henry William, in Woolwich in 1886; Florence, in Sheerness on the Isle of Sheppey in 1890; and Elsie Maud, in Harwich in 1892. When the family took up permanent residence in Dover, after Charles Houghton's discharge from the army in 1895, two more children were born: Jack Reuben in 1896 and Ellen Rebecca in 1900, fondly known as Nellie.

Obedience and loyalty to parents and family—these were important virtues in the upbringing of children. The Houghtons operated like most families in the late-Victorian period on what appeared to be a rigidly prescribed formula of interaction between parents and children. Outward manifestations of affection were almost nonexistent. Each child knew, to be sure, that he or she belonged within the network of the family; each knew, too, that he or she was expected to conform to an unwritten code of conduct which allowed for little freedom and spontaneity. It was the way things were supposed to be; their turn would come later, presumably, when they established their own homes. In the meantime, they were expected to respect the time-honoured traditional values and to honour and obey their parents and elders.

Nellie, the youngest daughter, now an octogenarian, says, "Our parents were good; we had a happy home life. They were strict in things that mattered: always to speak the truth, to help others whenever possible, and to respect their wishes."

The Houghton family circle was an unusually closed one. For some reason neither Charles Houghton nor his wife Martha maintained any contact with their relatives. Nellie recalls that her mother used to talk a lot about the Ellis family but, she said, "We never went to Ringmer, Sussex." The only relation she ever met was a cousin who was in the army and stationed in Dover during the First World War.

"I remember," she said, "he called at our place a few times, but what happened to him, I do not know." Her father used to kid about his being from Shakespeare's country, but she said the family never went there nor did they meet any of their father's relatives.

Even within the immediate family, relationships do not seem to have been very close-knit. The large gaps in the children's ages precluded sibling rivalry. When Nellie was born, the three oldest had already left home; by the time she was ten years old, she was the only member of the family still living at home. Moreover, moving from one military base to another made it virtually impossible for the older children to identify with any particular place and establish long-term friendships with other children. Accordingly, each member of the family took advantage of the first opportunity to leave home and pursue an independent career. Charles joined the army at the age of seventeen, Henry at the age of sixteen, and Jack went to Canada at age fourteen years.

The girls were in their mid-twenties when they married, and they dutifully followed their husbands—May to Scotland, Elsie to Canada. And so it was that the youngest unmarried girl, Nellie, was left to shoulder the responsibility of their aging parents. Within this undemonstrative family context, it is perhaps not surprising that Nellie was the sole mourner at the graveside of her parents when they were interred in St. James Cemetery, one in April, 1921, the other in November of the same year.

Obedience and loyalty to the Crown! In this regard, the Houghtons were faithful images of the English ideal. The three boys, like their father, served their country in one way or another thoughout their lives. The three girls, like their mother, performed conscientiously the tasks expected of Victorian women in the household and society-at-large.

Obedience and loyalty to the Church of England! These were taken for granted in the Houghton household. Martha Houghton saw that each of her children was promptly christened in the Anglican faith shortly after birth. During their formative years, the children were expected to attend Sunday school and the services of the Church of England on a regular basis. When the family settled in Dover, they were devoted members of St. James's parish. Their religious lives seem to have revolved around three books—the Bible, the Book of Common Prayer, and the Church of England hymnal. Among the cherished family memorabilia is a copy of this hymn book, *Hymns, Ancient and Modern*, which eighteen-year-old May gave Elsie on the occasion of her tenth birthday, and a King James Bible, which Martha Houghton gave her youngest daughter when she reached the age of twelve. The externals of religion, in the form of the rites of baptism, marriage and burial, continued to play a role throughout their later lives, but it was the more subtle Protestant work-ethic which seems to have had the greatest impact on the future endeavours of the Houghton men and women.

Devotion to duty was another epithet given top priority in the Houghton household. The sense of duty instilled from childhood propelled them as a matter of principle to do diligently what had to be done. This fidelity to the task of the moment developed in them a sense of their own self-worth which was conveyed by their very presence and bearing. But this same independence and self-assurance, born of a disciplined way of life, could be perceived as haughtiness and arrogance. As Elsie discovered, out of context, these traits could lead to misunderstanding and alienation, and it was this imperial style that earned her both respect and contempt in adulthood.

2 | The View from Cliffe Cottage

Three years before the Houghton family made Dover their permanent residence, Martha Houghton gave birth to her third daughter. This child was born just one year after thirteen-month-old Florence was buried in Sheerness on the Isle of Sheppey. The new baby girl was, therefore, a welcome addition to the family, helping fill the void left by her sister's premature death.

Although Charles had been transferred to Shoeburyness, his wife was permitted to remain in their married quarters at Harwich until the expected baby arrived. On April 1, 1892, Elsie Maud Houghton was born—a birthdate no one in the family would allow her to forget! An entry in the army register attests to the fact that she was baptized on April 17 in the parish of Saint Nicholas, Harwich. Before settling and establishing roots in Dover, the Houghton family took up residence at two more locations—Shoeburyness and Lydd.

When Elsie Maud was three years old, her father retired from the army with an honourable discharge, after almost a quarter of a century of service. An army pensioner at the age of forty-one with

a good record—"regular habits, good conduct, temperate"—
Charles Houghton had no difficulty obtaining employment as
Queen's Messenger in the Army Service Corps Quarters, Guilford
Battery. This job included modest living accommodations for him
and his family, so military barracks were finally exchanged for
more private, if more confined, living quarters. "Shaft Cottage" on
the East Cliff of Dover, better known as "Cliffe Cottage," was a
small house located on the cliff above Guilford Battery, below
Dover Castle.

There was a shaft in the cliff behind the cottage with steps leading
to Dover Castle above. This was designated for the exclusive use of
military officers. There were eighty-one stone steps leading from
Cliffe Cottage to the street below. According to Nellie, the postman
refused to climb the stairs, so the mail had to be collected at the
military headquarters on Waterloo Crescent.

Small though the cottage was, with four rooms, kitchen and front
porch, it did have the indoor conveniences of running water and
flush toilet. With the exception of two temporary moves (while the
building was being repaired)—one to Maxton, a suburb of Dover,
and one to Woolcomber Street at the foot of the castle—this cottage
was home to the Houghtons for more than twenty years. It was here
that Martha Houghton showed her ingenuity in the household arts;
here, too, in the plot of land adjacent to the cottage, that Charles
Houghton demonstrated his proficiency in gardening; and it was
here that the two youngest children were born. It was at Cliffe
Cottage that the Houghton boys entertained their military friends
during the Great War. Cliffe Cottage was home to Elsie Maud
throughout her childhood and adolescence and, more importantly,
it was here that she met the Canadian soldier around whom her
mature life revolved.

By the time Elsie Maud reached school age, she was not eligible
to attend the military school at Dover Castle as her father was no
longer in active service. Consequently, she was enroled in the
Church of England school administered by the local council, St.
James's Elementary School for Girls near the old St. James's Church.
For some reason—whether of a trivial or serious nature—Elsie
Maud met with some difficulty at the school. Her mother, always
quick to defend her children, especially when there was a principle
at stake, promptly removed her daughter from the school and
registered her at a nearby private school on Castle Street, directed
by Miss Pay, a real Victorian lady—strict, but kind and patient.

Although younger brother Jack later attended the St. James's Elementary School for Boys, Nellie, the youngest, was enroled at Miss Pay's.

The experience of living at Cliffe Cottage was an education in itself and opened up for the Houghton children vistas far beyond those acquired from formal schooling. From the vantage point on the cliff, the whole panorama of Dover's architecture lay below them. Unlike most residents and the many thousands who pass through Dover, the Houghton family was sensitized to the beauty of the town and harbour below Cliffe Cottage, and to the castle on the heights above. Dover—town, castle, port—was an open history book which the Houghtons assimilated unconsciously as part and parcel of daily living.

The most impressionable years of Elsie's life were spent in this historically unique military and naval town. The castle provided the back-drop of her everyday experiences, and on the cliffs and downs, the relics of the stone, bronze and iron ages, the graves of Britons who fought with Caesar, as well as the Roman, Saxon, Norman and English monuments, represented the history of her native country, before her eyes, and under her feet. Three buildings, in particular, within the environs of the castle walls were signficant landmarks—the heavily-fortified Norman keep, located immediately above Cliffe Cottage, and the Roman *pharos* or lighthouse, the tallest surviving Roman structure in Britain, and the Saxon church of St. Mary-in-the-Castle where Dovorians assembled on Sunday mornings to watch the military parade on the castle grounds.

Access to the barracks and fortifications of the Western Heights was from Snargate Street, at the foot of the citadel. The Grand Shaft featured a 365-step triple staircase. This shaft, unlike the one leading to Dover Castle, was used as a convenient route for soldiers and other workers. Nellie recalls the colourful array of the military in dress uniform as they emerged from the shaft on Snargate Street. They marched along the esplanade, past Waterloo Crescent and Marine Parade, to East Cliff. The Houghtons could watch this spectacular sight without leaving home.

The massive harbour with its distinctive curved seafront promenade was another striking feature of Elsie's home town. How often did she look down over Admiralty Pier and watch the ocean-going, cross-channel vessels come and go from the port, conveying their cargoes and millions of passengers?

Some of the monuments for which Dover is noted were constructed while Elsie was a young woman. There was, for example,
the Bleriot Memorial, the granite aeroplane inlaid in the turf behind
Dover Castle. At seventeen, Elsie was probably an eyewitness to
the pioneer flight made across the English Channel on July 25, 1909,
by the French aeronautical engineer Louis Bleriot. Nellie and two
other ladies from Dover recall going to Northfall Meadow at 4 a.m.
the following day to view the plane. Less than a year later, two
seafront monuments were erected on East Cliff Promenade—the
Honourable Charles Stewart Rolls Memorial to commemorate the
first return flight across the English Channel by Charles S. Rolls,
and the Captain Matthew Webb Memorial commemorating the first
person to swim the Channel from Calais to Dover in August 1875.

There were a number of other landmarks which had great significance for the teenage Elsie. The three-hundred-year-old town hall
located on High Street in downtown Dover had a brilliantly
adorned hall which was used for dances among other activities.
Being a ballroom dancer, Elsie would have frequented that building. Nellie recalls that her sister was a beautiful seamstress and
made the dress she wore to her first dance. Other centres of entertainment were the Hippodrome, with its entrance on Snargate
Street, the Music Hall in Market Square, and the old familiar skating
rink located close to Cliffe Cottage. When the rink was demolished
after the outbreak of the war to make space for the Royal Air Naval
Base, the landscape of the Houghton's home town was already
beginning to change.

Dover was the town which Elsie identified as "Home Sweet
Home", at least her childhood home. In later years, reference to the
white cliffs of Dover evoked feelings of nostalgia, as memories of
her youth were sharpened and distilled.

When Elsie first left Dover, she was in her twenty-first year. Like
other girls of her age and status, she had been employed as a
domestic servant in her own home town ever since she completed
her formal schooling. As a teenager, she witnessed many emotional
farewells as one after another of her siblings left home. May, eight
years her senior, was married on April 20, 1908, in St. Martin's
Church, Chentow, Kent. On June 13 of the same year, her oldest
brother Charles moved to Canada. He had not been living at home
for the ten years he served with the Royal Artillery in England,
South Africa and the island of Saint Helena; nevertheless, his transfer to the permanent force of the Canadian Artillery had a ring of

finality to it. When he did return to England in the fall of 1910, he did so for the purpose of marrying his South African girlfriend Matilda Sarah Craig. Arrangements had been made for fourteen-year-old Jack to return with them to Canada where a job as a drill boy with the Canadian Pacific Railway was awaiting him in Montreal.

After his departure, Nellie, eight years her junior, was the only Houghton child living at Cliffe Cottage. A third brother Harry had not lived at home since he joined the Royal Artillery some years before. When he left the military in 1912, he took a position with the police force in Sheffield, South Yorkshire, and remained in the area until he enlisted with the Canadian Artillery in 1915. Meanwhile, because of her proximity to home, Elsie was expected to shoulder more and more responsibility for her parents and young sister.

Little is known of Elsie's life during this period, other than the information gleaned from reminiscences of her younger sister, inferences from family photographs, and general knowledge about home life in the Houghton family. Nellie expressed a feeling of admiration for her big sister.

> Elsie was exceptionally good to me, during those years when I was the only member of the family living at home.... Elsie was home in my first years, but as there is such a gap in our ages she was always grown up to me. She was a most wonderful sister, generous, bought me a number of expensive gifts even though she did not earn a lot of money. I cherish, in particular, a gold chain and pendant and a gold signet ring. She took me to musicals and dance performances. She was a beautiful seamstress and made me fancy underclothes. During the war she made me pajamas to wear in case of an air raid.

Photos of Elsie taken in her late teens and early twenties suggest that she was a sophisticated young woman with highly developed talents in the areas of grooming, dressmaking and tailoring. One, for example, taken at the age of eighteen when she was bridesmaid at her brother Charles's wedding, depicts a young lady with a mature, well-rounded look and pompadour hairstyle. Her gown reflects the Edwardian bell-form skirt with hemline flare, bodice trimmed with lace, bishop-style sleeves, sash at the waist and a high, throat-encasing collar. The severity of line is offset by the lace trim which adds an overall feminine touch. A later photo shows her proficiency in tailoring.

Sewing may well have provided a natural means of escape when Elsie was home, in the company of a demanding and domineering mother, in what appears to have been a loveless environment. It was no secret that her father consistently sought refuge from a scolding wife in a nearby pub. Small wonder, then, that Elsie, applied for a position as a temporary nurse at the London County Asylum, as a chance to get away from home.

The asylum to which Elsie made application was originally known as the Middlesex Lunatic Asylum, but more popularly referred to as the Hanwell Asylum. It was located in the district of Southall, approximately eight miles from central London. The institution, which was over eighty years old in 1913, had been designed initially for three hundred patients and had been world famous during the first twenty-five years of its existence. When Elsie began work, there were over twenty-five hundred patients and the so-called "monument to humanity" was going through its darkest period; morale is reputed to have been at an all-time low. The major change in over a half century was the addition of new buildings to accommodate the ever-increasing number of patients and personnel.

The buildings, which originally occupied three sides of a quadrangle, had been enlarged over the years. The structure was brick; the design, simple. The only attempt at ornamentation was reserved for three octagonal towers. The central tower was used for administrative purposes; the western wing with its built-in airing grounds for female patients; and, the eastern wing, including airing grounds and bowling green, for male patients. Each of these wings was classified in wards according to the extent of the patient's affliction. The Hanwell Hospital was well equipped to pioneer in occupational therapy, an approach that was recognized worldwide.

The staff register for the years 1875 to 1914 and the report from the engineers' department for the same period suggests that the institution was being run like a small town when Elsie was initiated to a career in nursing. It was a self-sufficient community. Those patients who were able to work were expected to contribute their services to the smooth running of the hospital.

Elsie Houghton was one of the young woman hired to help alleviate a stressful situation brought about by ill-health among the staff. Recommendations from her former employers and an interview with Dr. Bailey satisfied the sub-committee responsible for hiring that she had the necessary qualifications—that she was "a person of good moral character and intelligence, with a temperament adapted to the care of mentally ill patients, naturally and by training."

She began work on February 18, 1913, her annual salary being nineteen pounds, ten shillings. She was expected to wear a uniform provided by the hospital. It was a white estamene dress, an apron of linen duck and a cap. Elsie was obviously pleased with this new image because she promptly had a studio photo taken. When they were outdoors with patients, they wore three-quarter length scarlet capes, also provided.

Despite the efforts made in the nineteenth century to establish a training program, there was no formal preparation for nursing personnel when Elsie was hired; it was a classic case of learning by doing. Elsie learned from the older attendants what they knew, and she was expected to pick up other essential knowledge and skills from doctors and her own experience on the job. Guidelines had been in place in the third quarter of the nineteenth century which reflected Victorian policy for the care of the so-called lunatics.

> The attendants are to take pains to acquire a knowledge of the character of the patients, to encourage them to good conduct, to promote a return to habits of neatness and order, and to obtain their confidence by friendly treatment and uniform attention to their comforts. They must endeavor to promote such habits in the dirty patients as may prevent their being negligent of cleanliness when in bed, which may often be done by proper attention paid the last thing at night. They are to report to the physician or surgeon any particular circumstance coming to their knowledge respecting any of their patients, and especially if connected with their state of health or showing any return to reason.[1]

Whatever the expectations in 1913. Elsie fulfilled the six-month probationary period and continued to work on the nursing staff. She must have been identified as a valuable person for, as a rule, temporary help was let go after the emergency was over.

No comparable statement was found describing the conditions under which employees operated in 1913, It is possible, however, to reconstruct from hospital records a fairly accurate account of the daily routine duties, of management-labour relations, and the general morale of the work force. The staff register, for instance, records meticulously the names and birth dates of all employees, their marital status, the date of joining the service, the date the appointment was established, the specific assignment with a particular category of job, the wages offered and, where applicable, the date of leaving the service.[2] Since male and female staff were not permitted to associate within the walls of the hospital, there were male and female officers and servants, permanent and temporary staff. The "established female officers" in 1913 were the matron, the first assistant, the laundry mistress, the washroom mistress, the head nurse and the head night nurse. The servants were categorized for the most part as nurses and housemaids. The former included first- and second-class nurses, ward attendants, and temporary nurses; the latter, such jobs as assistant cook, assistant messwoman, laundry maid, kitchenmaid, and staff maid. All female staff were either unmarried or widows. All were expected to live in residence.

Temporary staff were not immune to the many illnesses which prevailed in the work place. A month after Elsie began work she too fell victim to one of the ailments and was confined to sick bay for a week; according to the record she was laid up for another week in July. Fortunately for Elsie, payment was granted to temporary nurses for the time they were off duty, invalided, with full pay for the first week of their absence and half pay thereafter, less any amount they received under the National Insurance Act. By the fall of 1913, illness among the staff, especially such serious illnesses as pulmonary tuberculosis and scarlet fever, had escalated to the extent that changes in living conditions and training were imperative. Semi-basement rooms were no longer to be used for sleep areas and nurses were permitted to sleep out of the residence on a temporary basis in lodgings approved by the committee.

Probationers were to be given a more structured period of training for twelve months, instead of six months, and confirmed in their positions if they fulfilled the year's requirements. Occasional lectures were replaced by an organized study program. This meant attendance at classes to the satisfaction of the medical superintendent and proof of proficiency in the content. Besides, they were expected to take the St. John's Ambulance course, to pass the pulmonary examination of the Medico-Psychological Association and purchase two certificates, one from the Nurses' Association, the other from the Medico-Psychological Association.

When these changes were implemented, Elsie chose not to enrol in the newly structured training program leading to the rank of second-class nurse; instead, she applied for the position of housemaid. Why she made this decision is not clear, as she had already proven herself under the old rules of the asylum and was qualified as a practical nurse. Whatever her reason, Elsie was hired as laundrymaid on November 1, 1913 and six months later was confirmed in that position.

It may be only coincidental that this decision to take a lesser position came on the heels of an incident listed in the minute books of the subcommittee. It involved a confrontation with the administration. The first assistant medical officer reported to the sub-committee:

> Housemaid Elsie Houghton entered the service 18th February, 1913. On May 23, 1915, she went away for her weekly day's leave and failed to return but sent a telegram to say her mother was ill and she had to nurse her. I wrote her on the 27th May asking for a medical certificate of her mother's illnesss. She returned to duty on May 31 without a medical certificate and told me that her mother had not been ill enough to need a doctor. She has already had a week's sick leave this year in April after a severe cold, and yet grumbled to me on May 31 that her annual leave is long overdue, which is not a fact. It can be easily understood that this may be taken as a precedent by other members of the staff, who desire to take a few days holiday. I have therefore reported the matter to the Committee for their decision.[3]

Elsie had been brought before the Committee on the fourth of June. The account of that meeting reads as follows:

> … on being seen [Elsie] stated that when she went home on occasional leave she found her mother in a very depressed condition. She had four brothers serving with the forces of the Crown, and as no news had been received for some time from two of them, her mother was considerably upset and she did not like to leave her. She had now arranged for a sister to be with the mother.

The Committee resolved the matter in a straightforward manner:

> In view of the special circumstances Housemaid Elsie Houghton be granted special leave of absence without pay for the time she was looking after her mother.

The chairman, however, made a special point of warning Elsie that she must not stay away again without permission! Devotion to duty came first here as elsewhere.

This incident confirms that Elsie was an independent, even aggressive individual, who was not intimidated by her superiors. Her job at the hopsital was probably very highly-valued for the advantages it offered in the way of independence, and its value greatly outweighed the occasional disgrace in confronting the authorities. In addition, this infraction is the occasion that coincided with the days prior to John Sark's departure for the front. Her mother's emotional health was the perfect alibi for her romantic interests. All things considered, the rebuke from the chairman of the committee and the loss of one week's wages was a small price to pay for the pleasure of the company of John Sark, the week before he left for the front.

3 | "In Sickness and in Health..."

On May 30, 1915, Elsie Houghton bid John Sark an affectionate farewell and Godspeed as he left for overseas action, only two months since their first meeting. Elsie, herself, had mixed feelings seeing him go. On the one hand, British girls from all ranks of society were being commended publicly for furthering the war effort by showing pride and admiration for their escorts in khaki. Journalists were doing their job by trying to make the war look good as they recounted in the newspapers the brave deeds of the army, navy, and airforce. On the other hand, Elsie knew from the vantage point of her home and from her family the stark realities of the war: guarded docks, darkened streets, uniformed men, torpedoed boats, missing planes, disabled soldiers; the published casualty list was a veritable telltale.

An important factor in her decision to remain at Hanwell was the knowledge that service rendered there was recognized as an important part of the war effort. Indeed, the administration was given authority to refuse an employee permission to join the naval or military forces if his or her services were considered indispensable. The London County Asylum did not minister directly to the military during the First World War; instead, it opened its doors to long-term patients who were evacuated from other London hospitals to make room for war casualties. As many as five hundred additional patients were accommodated at the asylum during each of the war years.

As Elsie went about her daily tasks at Hanwell, she was more alert than ever to the war news, particularly reports from the combat zone. As the days, weeks and months passed she would have learned that the remainder of the boys in the original second Canadian contingent, who were still training in the vicinity of Folkestone after John's departure, had crossed the channel in September to join the first Canadian contingent in the Ypres sector. She must have experienced in the very depths of her being the anxieties so ably described years later by Vera Brittain in her *Testament to Youth*. [1]

It was during this period of uncertainty that Elsie formed the habit of accompanying her Irish friend, Margaret Dunne, to Mass and other devotions at the nearby Roman Catholic Church of Our Lady and St. Joseph in Hanwell. Her faith in God seems to have called her towards the Roman Catholic Church, but not as a rebellion from her Church of England upbringing. Her youngest son Charlie recalls that his mother claimed she had deep faith in God, His providence, and prayer long before she was formally confirmed in the Catholic Church. This seed of faith seems to have found nourishment in the devotional exercises of the pre-Vatican II Roman Catholic Church. It was, however, the example and encouragement of her friend Margaret Dunne that expedited her decision to begin instructions in the Catholic faith.

Periodic letters from John and from her brothers brought some comfort to Elsie and her family. Then came the news that John Sark had been wounded while serving with the Seventeenth Battalion and taken by the Canadian Field Ambulance to the Second Stationary Hospital. Two days later his neck and chest wall were operated on at the Eighth Station Hospital, Wimereux, France, an operation which left him with a scar on the left side of his neck.

John's own version of events was recorded many years later:

> The wheel of a gun carriage fell upon my chest, shattering my constitution and affecting my heart to the point where I became utterly helpless. This turn of events was depressing because when I underwent physical examination upon arriving in England the doctor called three of his assistants to observe my condition. "This man,"

he said, "has a perfect heart, the finest in the Canadian contingent. I have never heard the equal of its beat." The gun carriage got me; otherwise, I was unscathed and in the mood for war.[2]

He was invalided back to England on board the hospital ship H.S. *Cambria* and reached the Bevan Military Hospital, Sandgate, on November 20. Back in England he was assigned to Shorncliffe, pending preparation for hospital. Nellie has a vivid recollection of accompanying her sister to visit John at Sandgate, just outside Folkestone, when he returned from France. "It was a big house in a side street taken over for the war," she said.[3]

For the next seven months Elsie followed the progress of her loved one from one English hospital to another—Monks Horton, Canterbury and Epsom. The last was a residential town in north central Surrey, known for its medicinal springs—an ideal location for convalescence; it was just fourteen miles southwest of London.

Elsie was greatly encouraged when on March 22, 1916, John was permitted to visit Buckingham Palace and to attend a concert for wounded sailors and soldiers given in the presence of the King and Queen. The entertainment included comedians and dancers, soloists, skits, the Empire Theatre Chorus and a program of songs by the choristers of the Temple Church assisted by the male voice choir formed specifically for music in war time.[4]

Another opportunity to visit London was occasioned by a letter of introduction to the Aborigines Protection Society which he received from his parish priest, Father John A. McDonald, Indian Commissioner for the province of Prince Edward Island. The group not only welcomed John Sark, but invited him to attend their next committee meeting. The secretary of the society wrote the following to Father McDonald:

> I am glad to say that he [Bombardier J. Sark] was able to get leave to come up to London from Epsom … the President and Committee were greatly interested in receiving him and hearing what he could tell us about the Micmac Indians and the Lennox Island Reserve, and of his own experiences at the front and in hospital…. His manly demeanor and frank manner impressed us very favorably.[5]

At some point in their relationship John Sark must have told Elsie something about his home and his people. Lennox Island was a place of natural beauty; the Micmac Indians were a happy people with a great respect for nature and a contemplative approach to life.

John was a romantic and had a way of fascinating people with his charm, his personality, and his fluency with words. His nostalgic description of the Indians in Atlantic Canada may well have conjured up in Elsie's mind a vision of the seventeenth-century American romance of the Indian "Princess" Pocahontas and the Englishman John Rolfe from the United States. Pocahontas, daughter of the Chief of the Powhaton tribe of the Algonquin Indian Nation was, for Virginians, what her name signified literally— "a bright stream between two hills"—inasmuch as she was instrumental in bringing about toleration and goodwill between the Anglo-American races some three centuries ago.[6]

Whether Elsie fantasized her relationship with John as a mirror image of this American love saga is a moot point. Some of her lifelong friends say that Elsie thought she was marrying a prince, that John Thomas Sark was king of Prince Edward Island. According to her grandniece Eleanor Callow:

> The last time I saw my aunt, we talked about Uncle John. She missed him very much. She had read a lot about far away lands and she spoke about leaving England and how disillusioned and shocked she was on her arrival on Lennox Island. She thought her father-in-law was Chief of Prince Edward Island, and she had established a little kingdom in her own mind.[7]

Whatever her thoughts and dreams may have been, she continued to visit John Sark whenever possible throughout his seven-month period of convalescence.

The First World War was a time when traditional social barriers were definitely down, when young people from different backgrounds were able to form close ties. For Elsie, an inter-racial, cross-cultural relationship would have been well-nigh impossible in peace-time. Above all else, she could convince herself of the pragmatic necessity that John Sark, a Canadian alone in England, was now a war casualty who needed a nurse, and she was there to fill that need.

On June 22, 1916, John was judged to be fit for full duty and was transferred to the Reserve Battery of the Canadian Forces Artillery in Folkestone. He was pleased to be stationed once again at Shorncliffe. He now knew that the Second Contingent of Canadian Artillery was far more fortunate in their headquarters at Shorncliffe

Camp than was the First Contingent at Salisbury Plain. He had learned early that

> Shorncliffe is the greatest artillery camp in Great Britain, and is the headquarters of that branch of service. It is a most pleasantly situated spot on a tract of country overlooking the English Channel on a height of land known locally as the Downs, between Folkestone and Dover, and virtually in sight of the French coast. Unlike Salisbury Plain, it is a permanent camp, with properly laid out and paved roads and comfortable buildings, and has target ranges which extend for several miles along the Downs. Overlooking the sea are a number of concealed forts, which mount guns of heavy calibre.[8]

On Sundays the servicemen liked to take advantage of the public baths and the hospitality of the people. It was well known that "the girls about Folkestone [were] crazy over the Canadians," and numerous invitations to dinner and supper were extended to Canadian soldiers.

Now, more than a year after his supper invitation at Cliffe Cottage, he realized that life in the camp would not be the same. The boys of the Twenty-third and Twenty-fourth Batteries had long since vacated Moore Barracks; the Third Division was preparing to go to the front. Furthermore, the Dover area was being subjected to heavy air raids. On June 23 a bomb destroyed the roof of the Red Lion Inn on Saint James Street. It was fortunate that Elsie's father was not there at the time. Conditions were so bad that the caves in Trevanion Street were opened and used as shelters. Cliffe Cottage was no longer a safe place to visit. Before things got worse, while he was relatively secure in his temporary placement with the Reserve Unit, he realized that this would be an ideal opportunity to propose marriage.

The opportunity to marry must have seemed like the chance of a lifetime for the twenty-four-year-old Elsie. She was deeply in love with John Sark and was ready and willing, even eager, to share the rest of her life with him, far from the confining and restraining atmosphere of home. Her spontaneous affirmative and definitive response to his proposal, despite opposition from her family, was a grace for which John Sark would never cease to thank God.

The potential obstacle to their marriage had been removed when, thanks to Margaret Dunne's influence, Elsie had decided to convert to Catholicism. She was aware that her family, and particularly her mother and her oldest brother, would be upset by her decision to

marry a Roman Catholic, but this did not deter the now independent Elsie. Accordingly, she was baptized "conditionally" on
November 10, 1916, by Reverend William O'Brien in the Church of
Our Lady and St. Joseph, Hanwell. Sponsors were not deemed
necessary as she had already been validly christened as an infant.

Meanwhile, John requested the necessary permission from his
military superiors and on November 26 was "granted permission
to marry without expense to the public." Elsie gave notice of her
intent to resign from the Hanwell Hospital and terminated her
contract with that institution on December 9.[9] As she was leaving
"with intention to marry," by the terms of the Asylum's Officers'
Superannuation Act of 1909, she was entitled to the return of her
contribution to the pension fund. The date of the wedding was set
for December 23, while John was on leave.

The marriage was solemnized in the Roman Catholic Church of
Our Lady Help of Christians and St. Aloysius in Folkestone. Mar-
garet Dunne was bridesmaid and Canadian soldier William C.
Browne was best man. Also in the wedding party were Elsie's sister
Nellie and Joe Parker. Nellie recalls that they had photos taken at
the George Marsh studio in Folkestone and the wedding reception
was held at the bride's home in Dover. According to John's
Canadian pay book, his cheques were henceforth payable to Mrs.
Elsie Sark, 24 Waterloo Crescent, Sea Front, Dover.

While her husband was stationed at Shorncliffe Camp, the new
bride was free to turn her talents and training more directly to her
own personal preferences—a course in midwifery and service of
those suffering from the effects of the war. Volunteers were being
recruited by the Red Cross Society and the Volunteer Aid Detach-
ment (V.A.D).

She was glad she had left the depressing atmosphere of Hanwell
Hospital. Tuberculosis(T.B.) had been on the rise each year since
she went to work there. In 1913 there were less than three hundred
cases of phthisis; by 1917, the number had almost tripled.[10] That
winter, 1916-1917, was a particularly severe one. Food was being
rationed, so diet was restricted. Worst of all, the hospital was overcrowded. So, for the time being—whether studying for further
qualifications, working in one of the many nursing institutions on
Waterloo Crescent, or assisting as a volunteer nurse in the environs
of war-torn Dover only a few miles from her husband's headquarters at Shorncliffe—she was grateful for the change.

On June 22, 1917, just one year after John's return to active duty, six months after their marriage, John Sark was assigned to the Second Brigade of the Canadian Reserve Battery at Shorncliffe, to be absorbed once again for active service in the field. One month later he was admitted as a patient to Admiral Moore Barracks, Canadian Artillery Regimental Depot (C.A.R.D.). The diagnosis indicated a tubercular lung. The accident and ensuing operation in France had indeed taken its toll! On September 19 the verdict was announced—a posting back to Canada for further medical treatment. The final outcome, Elsie learned later, was his assignment to the newly-constructed Dalton Sanatorium, North Wiltshire, Prince Edward Island.

It was a nerve-wracking farewell as the SS *Llandovary Castle* set sail for Halifax, Nova Scotia, on September 20, 1917. John's marriage to Elsie had been approved by the military on condition it would involve no expense to the public. Elsie decided she would bide her time before attempting to negotiate with the military authorities. One thing, to be sure, was non-negotiable—her determination to follow through the life-commitment on which she had embarked when she exchanged marriage vows with John J. Sark.

Six long months passed, however, before the young bride was permitted to leave the white cliffs of Dover, her family, friends, and country, to join John on the other side of the Atlantic Ocean.

Part Two
1918-1945

Intreat me not to leave thee, or to return from
following after thee: for whither thou goest, I will
go; and where thou lodgest, I will lodge: thy
people shall be my people and thy God my God.

The Book of Ruth, I: 16.

4 | Journey to the Island

The months following John Sark's return to Canada were hard ones for Elsie, left behind in war-torn England. On the one hand she knew from her own experience working among the T.B. patients at Hanwell Hospital that the mortality rate, especially among men, had quintupled in the years she had been there. On the other hand she was grateful to God that everything possible was being done to promote her husband's recovery.

Dalton Sanatorium, the hospital to which he was assigned, was a relatively new structure situated in North Wiltshire, about sixteen miles west of Charlottetown. It had been built through the generosity of philanthropist Sir Charles Dalton when, as president of the Anti-Tuberculosis Society, he became cognizant of the need for such an institution on Prince Edward Island.[1] The twenty-four-patient capacity sanatorium was opened in March, 1915, and a few months later it was taken over by the Military Hospitals Commission for the treatment of returned soldiers. Under the aegis of the federal government, the facility was expanded and equipped as a first-class tuberculosis hospital. Photographs of the structure assured Elsie that the building was very attractive from the exterior; John's description of the interior facilities, health services, and rest program was a source of great satisfaction to her. Had she known or even surmised the doctors' prognosis for John, she would never have delayed going to him for so long.

As it happened the winter of 1917-1918 was severe both in Canada and the United Kingdom. The long, lonely days and the threatening environment—the anti-aircraft gunfire, the explosions of bombs, the cries of wounded soldiers—became more and more depressing for the heartsick Elsie. She managed to drag herself through the daily rounds of regular and volunteer work in an efficient but somewhat anesthetized manner. She was particularly alert to news relating to the four divisions of Canada's artillerymen, and was able to recount in her letters to her invalid husband information about the men of the Canadian Expeditionary Force which she gleaned from her brother Harry and the British news media. She was thankful that her husband's life had been spared, even though her heart ached at the very thought of his helpless condition. Important dates came and went uncelebrated—John's twenty-ninth birthday, the first anniversary of her acceptance into the Catholic Church, their first wedding anniversary, Christmas, New Year's—and still there was no word of John's release from hospital. She was well aware that the Canadian government assumed no financial responsibility for the wives of soldiers who married after enlisting in the army. However, John did obtain the necessary permission to marry her; surely they had a moral obligation to keep her informed of his condition.

After six long months of waiting Elsie decided to take the matter into her own hands. Early in 1918, she applied to the British authorities for permission to join her husband in Canada. Her intention, she told them, was to become a permanent citizen of Canada. She explained that with her background training, experience and expertise in working with T.B. patients, she could expedite her husband's recovery. Her plan to surprise John was thwarted when the Canadian authorities asked for some assurance that her husband was able to support her. "Where you are," she wrote to him, "I should be. Do you want me to come?" His reply to Elsie was a prompt and unconditional "Yes"; to the authorities, "Send her to me!"

Despite the conflicting news reports from the front, Elsie's spirit was in tune with the unusually warm spring weather that had finally descended on England. She went about the last-minute preparations for departure without giving too much thought to the significance of her decision. She was advised that she would be sailing for Halifax, Nova Scotia, from Liverpool on March 13. The transport ship, SS *Olympic* would be sailing under the white ensign with about 7,000 passengers on board, all of whom were associated, in one way or another, with the Canadian Expeditionary Force. She knew from her brothers Jack and Charles that Canadian winters are cold, but as she was scheduled to arrive in Canada on the first day of spring, she decided to dress appropriately for that season. So, she carefully packed her heavy clothing and decided to wear a lightweight navy-blue spring suit, topcoat and dress shoes.

The most difficult part of leaving, the one thing she dreaded, was the farewell to family and friends. Both parents were already in their sixties and her three brothers were in the thick of battlefields in France. Should anything happen to any one of them, the burden of responsibility would ultimately fall on the shoulders of teenage Nellie; her older sister May had her own husband and family to worry about. However, there was no turning back. It was her duty to go now, and she would set emotion aside, and when the time came, assume a strong stance and do what duty, her upbringing and her conscience dictated. At the same time, her parents were steeling themselves for the dreaded day of Elsie's departure.

Both parents were at the Dover Station to wish their daughter Godspeed. The optimistic Elsie, for her part, tried to reassure them that all was well, that even though the war was at its height, she would be safe. There were no bands playing, no fanfare signalling the train's departure as Martha Houghton stood stoically beside her husband, with Nellie close by, watching as Elsie stepped out into an uncertain future.

Elsie was probably experiencing mixed feelings as she travelled first to London, then after changing stations, on to Liverpool. The fact that her husband was ill and needed her was the real rationale for the voyage, she told herself. Nevertheless, leaving her parents in such a vulnerable locale, as well as the separation from her childhood home were the cause of some doubts and heartache.

Crossing the Atlantic took just one week, but the foul weather and the steerage accommodations contributed to a depressing experience at sea. After the steamer arrived in Halifax at 3 p.m. on March 20, instead of disembarking at once, passengers were required to remain on board until medical and civil examiners Drs. Arn O. Morton and F.W. Hetherington gave them clearance. The steamer docked at 1:30 p.m. on March 21, and steerage passengers were examined that afternoon. That meant an extra two nights aboard ship. Less than four months prior to Elsie's arrival in Halifax, the city had been almost levelled by a terrific explosion when two ships, one carrying a cargo of TNT, the other a relief ship, collided in the Bedford Basin as they moved through the Narrows, the approach to the harbour.

So, when she disembarked, there was not even a railway station! The old North Street Station had been demolished and the new modern one to be linked with a deluxe hotel as well as the new ocean terminal were still in the planning stage.

On learning there were three "specials" ready to carry passengers from the steamer to various points throughout Canada, she located the Intercolonial train which would connect with the train for her destination.

Prince Edward Island, she learned, was Canada's smallest but most densely populated province. It consisted of 2,184 square miles and had a population of approximately 100,000. It was difficult for her to relate to these facts. The county of Kent in south-eastern England from which she hailed had an area of 1,525 square miles, three-fourths the size of Prince Edward Island. Its population numbered one and one-half million. Her own home town of Dover had a population close to 50,000 and the town of Hanwell, where she worked, was roughly equivalent in population to that given for the entire Island. Yet, it was her understanding that the Island was self-governing, had its own governor and legislature, its own premier and cabinet. The French had named it Île Saint-Jean; the English had re-christened it Prince Edward Island in honour of Edward, Duke of Kent; but, much earlier on, the Micmac Indians had ascribed to it the name Abegweit, meaning "Cradled on the Waves." She smiled as she recalled the legend of how her husband's people came to Prince Edward Island in the first place; it was part of the Micmac Indians' version of the Creation story.[2]

Allegedly, Prince Edward Island was also referred to by non-Indian Islanders as "the garden of the Gulf" and "the million-acre farm" because of its pastoral simplicity, its balmy air and its prolific soil. The enchanted land of Anne of Green Gables fame was reputed to have all the features of utopia! In a few hours she herself would be in a position to separate fact from fiction.

Despite depressing weather conditions, the ride on *terra firma*, though tiring, was a welcome change. The trip from Halifax, north through the center of Nova Scotia to the industrial town of Amherst, and across the New Brunswick border to the quiet, university town of Sackville, took roughly four-and-a-half hours. Here, Elsie transferred from the Ocean Limited to the Canadian National Railway train which carried her along the southern part of New Brunswick, over the thirty-six miles of track to the new ferry terminal at Cape Tormentine.

This steamship service between Cape Tormentine and Port Borden which began operations in October 1917, virtually connected Prince Edward Island with the mainland by rail. Furthermore, it established the desperately-needed freight, passenger, mail and express service which had been promised the Island province when it joined the Confederation of Canada some forty-five years before.

This winter, however, was one of the worst years for interruptions in transportation. Fortunately, there were no serious delays in the train and ferry service this unseasonably cold, raw March day, so the ferry made the nine-mile crossing in approximately forty-five minutes. Before beginning the final thirty-mile stretch of track to North Wiltshire, Elsie caught a brief glimpse of the town of Borden, named after Canada's wartime premier, Sir Robert Borden. The run from Port Borden to Emerald Junction was just about one hour, and the final portion of the journey to North Wiltshire was roughly another hour.

The train moved through the villages of Breadalbane, Fredericton and Hunter River, with a view of gentle, undulating land and a sense of peace everywhere. The three-mile trek from the railway station to Dalton Sanatorium gave Elsie a closer look at the famous red soil of the Island. Unfortunately, her light top coat and walking shoes were no match for the weather and the mud. Fortified with prayer and determination, she found her way to Dalton and she walked into her husband's presence unannounced!

The travel-weary Elsie forgot momentarily her own physical discomfort. "Where you are, I should be," she repeated. "Here I am."

The unexpected arrival of John J.'s bride was a source of great excitement throughout the hospital. The administration, staff and patient body had come to know her vicariously through John and spontaneously they extended to her a reassuring welcome. Here, they noted, was a living example of courage and optimism. Arrangements were made quickly and quietly for her to remain at the hospital overnight. In Elsie's words, "the Charles Dalton Sanatorium was a beautiful place. I found my way there and stayed overnight."[3]

5 | Elsie's Island Home

A s soon as she could Elsie arranged to meet the doctors and nurses regarding the present state of her husband's health. She was not prepared to accept the report that his case was incurable, and made inquiries about the possibility of her assuming responsibility for her husband's convalescence. Accordingly, she encouraged John to apply for a discharge from the army. From that point on things began to happen!

He obtained permission from the hospital authorities to go to Charlottetown to arrange a temporary leave. His intent was to bring his bride to Lennox Island as soon as possible and introduce her to his people. They took advantage of the overnight visit to see some of the historic landmarks of Charlottetown, the birthplace of Canada, starting with the Provincial Building.

This historic site held fond memories for John. When he was just eight years old, he accompanied his family to Charlottetown to attend the celebration of Queen Victoria's Diamond Jubilee, during which his father was presented with a gold medal and watch. Close by was the new Gothic stone cathedral of St. Dunstan's, replacing the structure John had known during his college days which was totally destroyed by fire in 1913. The new edifice was not quite complete. Across the street from the cathedral was the Bishop's Palace, the residence of the Bishop and the clergy of the cathedral parish. On the outskirts of the city was John's alma mater, St. Dunstan's College, which had been incorporated within the past year, giving it the power to grant degrees.

In Charlottetown, Elsie had an opportunity to meet Father John A. McDonald, the priest who had taken an interest in John while he was invalided in England. Father John A., as he was called, was the Indian Agent for Prince Edward Island. He was also pastor of St. Patrick's Parish in Grand River which included the St. Anne Mission on Lennox Island and was, therefore, responsible for both the spiritual and temporal welfare of the Indians.

When he learned of the young couple's plans, he advised them to consider an intermediate move before taking up residence on the Reserve.[1] He pointed out to Elsie the potential difficulty of attempting to care for an invalid husband, while trying to adjust to a totally new environment. The parochial house in Grand River, he said, was immense and the two of them would be more than welcome to make a temporary home there. Elsie would be close enough to Lennox Island to cross over on the boat when weather conditions permitted and, in that way, gradually get to know the Indians before establishing a permanent residence on the Reserve. "No way!" she said. Her husband's people live on Lennox Island; that was where they should live. Undoubtedly, her military family background and Victorian upbringing had conditioned her for her duty as wife and homemaker; she would soon learn it was not the best preparation for the Micmac lifestyle!

The train journey from Charlottetown to Summerside, a distance of 48 miles, was a one-and-one-half-hour or a three-hour ride depending on whether one travelled on a "passenger" or a "mixed" train. John knew from his experience that mixed trains were best for seeing all the pleasant little villages along the way. This was an excellent opportunity for the young couple to be alone with each other. Since there was no train west of Summerside that evening, they probably travelled the more leisurely route. For the enthusiastic Elsie, the trip was akin to a honeymoon experience. As they chatted, they watched the Island countryside pass by—the hedgerows of spruce, the pasture land for grazing sheep and cattle, and the cultivated farm lands. After a night in Summerside, the young couple boarded the train for Port Hill, a distance of twenty-two miles. From there they would be transported by mailman Birchfield Swabey Birch along his route—a four-mile drive to the Tyne Valley and Port Hill post offices and across the one and a quarter-mile stretch of ice across Richmond Bay to Lennox Island. Ordinarily, spring was a hazardous time for crossing from the mainland to the island, but this was an unusually cold March day, and the bay was covered with ice. Elsie felt lighthearted and full of adventure as she mounted the horse-drawn sleigh waiting at the Port Hill railway station.

John, for his part, was eagerly anticipating the moment he would present his English bride to his father, the Chief, and to the Micmac community. Mailman Birch is reported to have remarked to his acquaintances that this self-assured, attractive lady would not remain long in that remote godforsaken place!

On reaching Lennox Island the driver followed the usual route up from the wharf, past the priest's house on the right and the imposing tall-spired church on the left, to the council house, a multi-purpose building which had served as post office for the Island for the past six years. As Elsie stepped down from the sleigh and into the building, she was taken aback by the formal reception awaiting them. All the Indians on the Reserve had been summoned and were sitting in a circle on the floor cross-legged, with their Chief in the centre. A look of magnificence emanated from Chief John Thomas Sark. Even before this striking figure advanced to welcome her with words of greeting and friendship, she instinctively read the sign of approval in his eyes. Little did she realize as she returned her father-in-law's gentle handshake that for him she represented the Crown and all that was good and honourable in the English tradition.

Gathered there no doubt in obedience to their beloved Chief, the Micmac Indians were an awesome picture. It was a far cry from what she expected. The men seated on one side were handsome, and with the exception of the Chief, most were slightly smaller build than the average Englishman. They were black-haired, black-eyed, clean-shaven and athletic-looking, like her husband. The physical characteristics of the women did not appear to be quite so clearly etched. Intermarriage with whites over the past three centuries had clouded the nascent Micmac features.

Her presence among them seemed to have evoked a reserve—or was it a natural bashfulness—which unnerved her, made her feel very uncomfortable. They were obviously pleased to see John J., and as he mingled among them, they seemed to converse easily. As the evening progressed, their conversation became more and more spirited. After all, she reflected, John had been the most eligible bachelor on the Reserve before the war! She could read their thoughts: why this woman—white, English, a stranger? She had the gut feeling that from their perspective, she was not good enough for John.

As she felt the pressure of her isolation. the Chief's radiant smile was reassuring. In all probability he commended her for her courage in crossing the Atlantic while the war was in progress. He was aware that her three brothers were even then serving as army officers on the firing lines in France. Her bravery had given new vitality to his invalid son and he hoped her presence would bring a ray of hope to those families on the Reserve whose men were also at the front. Very likely he spoke, too, of the honour bestowed on him by the late Queen and explained the significance of the three medals he was wearing. One was an heirloom, given to his ancestor by the French in about 1715; the second was a Diamond Jubilee gift; and the third was the medal of Pope Pius presented by the Archbishop of Montreal.

A mutual admiration seems to have developed that evening between the Chief and his English daughter-in-law, a relationship which lasted throughout their lives.[2]

Later that evening, the natty Elsie hastily put together a set of improvised curtains—a detail which did not go unnoticed and marked her off immediately as "uppish" by the local community.[3] She then carefully unpacked her delicate wedding gifts and stowed them away with the kid gloves she had considered an essential part of her wardrobe.

John sensed her feeling of despondency and tried to cheer her. His people, he assured her, were by nature warm, accepting, compassionate; if they seemed aloof and unfriendly to her, it was because they perceived her a stranger. When they came to know her, it would be different. However, he understood her feelings and promised she would not have to stay on Lennox Island any longer than was necessary, if that was her wish. As soon as he was given a clean bill of health he would seek employment with the Canadian National Railway in Moncton, New Brunswick. There she would be in a white community and relatively close to her brothers.

In the days following this formal reception to Lennox Island, Elsie wrestled with the contrasts—the warm greeting, the kind words of the Chief, set against the sense of mistrust from the general community. After wartime England, the peaceful open landscape of her new surroundings was also a prison of geographic, cultural and linguistic isolation.

Nevertheless, having withstood the shock of her first meeting with the Micmac band and having been assured that her sojourn on Lennox Island would be short-lived, Elsie was prepared, at least, to settle temporarily on the Reserve. She knew it was imperative that she learn as much as possible about the Indians and their relationship with the white community, before her husband's army leave expired. At that time, the history of the Micmacs and the changes that had occurred to their way of life was not well-documented, but John Sark could proudly tell what he knew from two perspectives—from his Micmac roots and his white education.

The Micmacs, the most eastern tribe of the Algonquin-speaking people and the dominant Indian group in the Maritime provinces of Canada, were the only inhabitants of the coastal region of the Gulf of St. Lawrence prior to French colonization; for centuries they were the sole occupants of what is now the province of Prince Edward Island.

Like other aboriginal tribes, the Micmacs enjoyed a spiritualized relationship with their environment.

> The world of the Micmac was ... filled with superhuman forces and beings (such as dwarfs, giants and magicians), and animals that could talk to man and had spirits akin to his own, and the magic of mystical and medicinal herbs—a world where even inanimate objects possessed spirits.
> Micmac subsistence activities were inextricably bound up within this spiritual matrix, which acted as a kind of control mechanism on Micmac land-use, maintaining the environment within an optimum range of conditions.[4]

This was a cosmology which called for responsibility in the preservation and development of the universe. Stewardship, not ownership, was the underlying concept which motivated the relationship of the aboriginal people to the land. This world-view was all but completely destroyed when, in the late eighteenth century, all the land on the island was confiscated by the imperial government. It was the climax of many changes that had been taking place in the Micmac *weltanschauung* and life-style for the four centuries following contact with Europeans and their culture.

The first record of contact is found in the journal of Jacques Cartier who made various reconnaissance landings on the north shore of Prince Edward Island on July 1, 1534, and claimed the land for Francis I, King of France. For almost two hundred years the island seems to have been a fisheries possession for French colonial interests in the fur trade and fisheries on a seasonal basis. During this period, prior to the arrival of the English, a close relationship developed between the native Micmac Indians and the French. By the early seventeenth century, when the French held the monopoly on the trading and fishing industries throughout Acadia, the Micmacs had adopted Christianity and were increasingly dependent on European trade. So intrigued were they by the similarities in the symbolism and ritualism used in the Christian religion with those used in their traditional religion that Chief Membertou and twenty of his braves were baptised at Port Royal, on the mainland, in 1610. That same year a concordant was signed directly with the Church of Rome which designated the Micmac nation a Catholic nation. By the terms of the agreement, French missionaries were permitted to come to Acadia and freely preach the Christian message.[5]

At the same time, the Micmac subsistence pattern was being radically changed by the fur trade, which, in turn, changed settlement patterns and re-oriented family relationships. Furthermore, their penchant for "fire water" (alcohol) made them vulnerable to economic exploitation.

Throughout the one hundred and fifty years of French-English conflict (1613-1763), tentative outposts gradually became permanent colonial settlements, and European control was extended over the lucrative trading, fishing, and land resources in the region. With the failure of the fur market, encroachment on Indian lands was followed by exploitation of the lands themselves. This made it difficult, if not impossible, for the natives to pursue their traditional hunting activities in Acadia.

During the period of the French regime (1720-1758), Île Saint-Jean (the French name for the island) continued to serve as an outpost for the fort at Louisburg. The first settlement had been established at Port La Joie (near present-day Charlottetown) in 1719, after the French king granted the island to Comte de Saint-Pierre, an influential Frenchman, for the purpose of carrying on the fisheries. This was the site chosen for assembling the Micmacs annually in June or July. Here they were feasted and presented with gifts, in return for which they were expected to pledge their loyalty to France. Meanwhile, the French population was growing steadily. According to J. Henri Blanchard, after about forty years, there were more than 25 villages and by the time of the Deportation of the Acadians in 1753, there were about five thousand inhabitants. They had cultivated more than 12 thousand acres of farmland.[6]

French missionaries ministered to the three hundred Indians living on Île Saint-Jean. With their assistance, the Micmacs remained faithful allies of the French. In joining with the French against the English, the Micmacs were helping to protect what they perceived to be their land. Thus, after the fall of Louisburg to the English in 1758, the Micmacs refused to surrender. It was only after the Crown issued a proclamation in 1763 which affirmed the Indians' legal title to the land —an agreement which could only be extinguished by a treaty with the Crown—that they were willing to pledge allegiance. This proclamation, they hailed as their Magna Carta! It not only ensured security of their lands and freedom to move from place to place as hunters and fishermen, but it also recognized their tribe as a nation with whom future negotiations were possible. However, no sooner was the ink dry on the parchment than, without consultation with the aboriginal people, the entire Island was divided in lots, and transferred at one stroke on one day to private ownership!

In 1764, just one year after the proclamation was signed and sealed, the British government commissioned Captain Samuel Holland to survey "St. John Island." He divided the island into sixty-seven townships or lots, and by means of a lottery, in London in 1767, the townships were handed over to a group of absentee British proprietors. The Micmacs, however, were left undisturbed on their traditional encampments for a number of years. When Lieutenant-Governor Walter Patterson became aware of the fact that the 1,320-acre offshore island situated off the northwest coast of St. John's Island had been overlooked in the lottery, it was attached to Lot 12 and granted to Sir James Montgomery in 1772. This island, named Lennox Island by Captain Holland in 1765, had been the favourite campsite of the Micmac Indians for centuries.

Despite numerous appeals made by the Indians to Patterson's successor, Lieutenant-Governor Edmund Fanning, for their own lands, with access to water, the only result was a loose arrangement with Montgomery for the Indians to reside on Lennox Island. Montgomery offered to sell it to the government, but the offer was ignored. By 1800, several Micmac families were established there; Lennox Island was seen as a safe refuge. With the assistance of a missionary priest Abbé de Callone, they established the mission of

St. Anne. They built a log chapel and the Micmac Indians congregated here each year to celebrate the feast of their patron saint. In 1806 the *abbé* petitioned the British government to buy the Island for the Micmac Indians. As the aboriginal owners, he said, they had the right to have at least some portion of their ancestral homeland. Nothing came of this petition. In 1834, when Bishop McEachern expressed the same interest on behalf of the Indians, he was informed that David Stewart of London had already purchased it for the stated purpose of "protecting the Indians and to prevent their being annoyed and driven about."[7] Four years later, Stewart was prepared to sell the island to the Colonial Office for £1,500, on condition that they provide security for the Indians. However, the assembly's survey showed that the land was not worth more than £200, so they did not vote the money.

The first legislative recognition came almost two decades later, on April 14, 1856, when a bill was passed providing for the appointment of commissioners of Indian affairs, whose duty was to protect Indian lands. The appointed commissioners were Theophilus Stewart and Henry Palmer, but the Micmacs of Prince Edward Island were officially landless! The commissioners made conscientious efforts to effect change but met with little, if any, co-operation from the government.

When the normal procedures to alleviate the plight of the Indians failed to evoke a response from the assembly, Commissioner Theophilus Stewart played what proved to be his trump card. In 1862 he founded the Micmac Society, expressly for assisting "the native Indians in rendering the cultivation of the soil an auxiliary to their ordinary manufacturing pursuits, and in forwarding the education of their rising generation."[8] As secretary of the society, he wrote to the Aborigines' Protection Society of London and described the distress of the Indians. In Britain, £400 was raised and negotiations for the sale of Lennox Island were completed on June 2, 1870. The title was invested in the trustees of that Aborigines' Protection Society until May 30, 1912, on which date the title was vested in King George V. This was the first formal claim the Indians had to Lennox Island as their own Reserve, and it was just six years prior to Elsie's arrival.

Meanwhile, after Confederation the administration of Indian Affairs, which had been under the management of the several provinces, came under the control of the Dominion of Canada, and responsibility for Indians' affairs was given to the Secretary of State.

In 1873, the year that Prince Edward Island entered Confederation, the Department of the Interior was created and within it, the Indian Branch. When the visiting superintendent reported to the Minister of the Interior in January 1875, there were 302 Micmacs on Prince Edward Island. They owned no real property other than the 1,320 acres on Lennox Island which was held in trust by the Aborigines' Protection Society, and the 204-acre tract on Township 39, held in trust for eight families. There were ten frame buildings, one solitary dilapidated log-house, and fifty-six "old-fashioned camps." Such was the legacy of the imperial government to the Micmacs of Prince Edward Island!

Under the Canadian government, the Micmacs of Prince Edward Island fared no better. Most of the lands granted them by private individuals were confiscated. The Victorian policy of relegating the Indians to Reserves was fully endorsed by the federal government. In practice, this meant that the Indians were not only cut off from their roots, but they were also denied access to the mainstream of Canadian society. The Lennox Island Reserve was not only isolated from the mainland of Prince Edward Island, it was ice bound for at least three months of each year. Thus, the Micmacs were prisoners in a land which was aboriginally theirs! In 1880, the Indian Department became a separate department, and the Indian Act of that year legally stripped the Micmacs of their economic base and imposed on them a totally alien bureaucracy. By the terms of this act,

> The Minister of Indian Affairs in Ottawa had responsibility for every one of a band's resources, including land, housing, capital and income, livestock and equipment, and he had ultimately authority over medical services, employment and education.... He was served by a bureaucracy consisting of provincial and regional superintendents, and an agent on every reserve who exercised near-dictatorial powers over the day-to-day life of the community. If an Indian wanted to leave the reserve for any reason, if he wanted to build a house or cultivate a piece of land he first had to ask the agent, who might take months reporting to and receiving a reply from Ottawa.[9]

The only way to escape from this paternalistic policy was by enfranchising and becoming a Canadian citizen. In effect this meant ceasing to be an Indian!

Despite the restrictive and oppressive measures imposed by a dominant white bureaucracy, the Micmacs of Prince Edward Island resisted attempts to keep them on the Reserves and to make them stationary farmers. Through the manufacture of baskets and other Indian wares, they earned starvation wages, moving from place to place and setting up campsites for the purpose of selling their handicrafts. They were able to supplement their meagre income by fishing and by seasonal migration to Maine for potato and blueberry picking. After the confiscation of their lands on Prince Edward Island, they did not lose their pride and independence, even though they were forced to live in poverty and in the most inhumane conditions.

Considering John Sark's pro-British sentiments after the war, one wonders whether he was capable of painting for his English wife a realistic picture of Micmac life. The Sark family had been honoured many times over by the Crown and its representatives. When John himself was singled out for distinction some years later, his personal sentiments became a matter of record. After reviewing the carefree lifestyle his forefathers enjoyed, he said:

> Fortunately, the life you whites had to offer us was a fuller and richer one than our old life of hunting and fishing. We have been provided with reserves of land on which to live. We are taking hold of this new life; we are tilling the soil as you do; our homes are like your homes; our life today is like your life. For 400 years our young people have been marrying your young people, and there is now little difference between us. Together with you we are striving to build up a new Canada.[10]

"Not anywhere," he said, "will you find more loyal subjects of King George."

It seems unlikely that this concept of "progress" in Indian-white relations reflected accurately the true feelings of the Micmac Indians as a group on Prince Edward Island. In retrospect, therefore, Elsie probably never understood the latent source of the deep-seated conflict she experienced repeatedly in her dealings with the Indians. It was not only that she embodied the white colonial community, she was now married to a member of the band who aligned himself in various ways with the white establishment.

6	The Lennox Island Reserve: 1918

For Elsie Sark, her husband's island home was a world far removed from her childhood home. Here on Lennox Island, there was no public transportation, no urban centre, no telephone. Contact with the mainland was weather dependent, and the area was more sparsely populated than she could ever have imagined while growing up in southeast England.

In fact, there were two main areas of settlement on the Reserve, in the southwest region and in the north.[1] Two main roads served these clusters of homes. Gull Point Road led from Chapel Point, in the southwest tip of the island where the wharf is located, along the south of the island to Gull Point on the southeast end. Cove Road led north from Gull Point Road, with large peat bogs clearly visible on either side. There were approximately forty families in these two regions along the main roads. They lived in frame houses, most of which were whitewashed and seemed in good repair. Indians in other parts of Prince Edward Island lived, for the most part, in temporary buildings—shacks, shanties, and wigwams. The interiors of the houses were clean but bare as compared with the average white home. The essentials were there: table, chairs, beds, cooking stoves and, perhaps, a clock, a battery radio, holy pictures and family photos. John's sister, Mary Elizabeth, had a sewing machine. Elsie must have been struck by the absence of colour and ornament; the drab interior of the homes reminded her of Hanwell Asylum.

When the census was taken in 1917 there were 292 Micmac Indians on Prince Edward Island, approximately two-thirds of whom lived on Lennox Island. The remainder were distributed among three reserves in the eastern sector of the province—Scotchfort, Morell, and Rocky Point. According to a report to the Department of Indian Affairs in 1916, 60 percent could speak English but only 40 percent could write the language; one person could speak and write French; close to 100 percent wore "civilized clothing."[2]

Although the number of males exceeded the number of females, there was a disproportionate number of adult women living on the Reserve when Elsie arrived because every able-bodied male had joined the armed forces. There were only 55 children attending the Indian day schools: 41 at Lennox Island, and 14 at the school recently opened in Rocky Point. A number of the Indian children were attending white schools on the mainland, especially in places where their parents had set up temporary camps, such as Richmond, Coleman, Freeland and Indian River. Some of the girls were attending the boarding schools in Miscouche and Tignish. Father John A. had worked hard for the school at Rocky Point because, as he reported,

> the Indians of Rocky Point are not allowed to send their children to the white school and are thus deprived of the benefits of education. Though efforts have been made with the assistance of the Superintendent of Education for the province, to have them admitted, these efforts have been so far unsuccessful. The grounds for the objection are that these children's parents are tubercular.[3]

Elsie was beginning to get the lay of the land!

The people, especially the women, she observed were hard-working and industrious. They supported themselves mainly by a combination of farming, fishing, hunting, and the manufacture of Indian wares. There were a few who held salaried positions which related directly to education and to the maintenance and servicing of the Reserve—the teacher, the school janitor, the truant officer, the ferryman. In general terms, Prince Edward Island prospered in 1916 and again in 1917, with progressive improvement in livestock, a booming fox industry and the new car-ferry transportation service; however, this affluence was not reflected on Lennox Island.

About ten small-scale farms were running on Lennox Island, primarily for sustenance. The land was not particularly good, and few people were strong enough to haul mussel mud for fertilizer. Of the more than 300 acres of cultivated Indian land, only sixty acres were under crop the past year. Individual farmers owned a total of twenty-six ploughs, harrows, drills, etc.; two binders; five wagons; about five hundred tools and smaller implements. These were often used when the Indians worked for white people in adjacent districts. The combined livestock for all those engaged in farming consisted of 9 mares, 2 foals, 9 milch cows, 1 bull, 2 steers, 4 young stock, and 135 poultry. They were encouraged to keep cows. Some income was earned from beef, over and above that used for local consumption. The Indians, Elsie observed, were very careful with the little stock and machinery they possessed.

The men were interested primarily in the traditional Indian occupations—fishing, hunting and trapping. During the summer months they fished cod and eel; in the autumn, oysters; in the winter, smelt; and in the spring, lobsters. The oyster fishery was a total failure during the fiscal year 1917-1918, and the lobster fishing was less profitable than the preceding season.

Hunting and trapping were favourite pastimes but had not been lucrative in recent years, even though as many as eight hundred geese were caught during the hunting season. There were twenty-five shotguns on the Reserve. Income from the industry did not reflect the value of furs on Prince Edward Island generally.

The most lucrative industry was the home manufacture of Indian wares: potato baskets, butter churns, wash tubs, axe-handles, hockey sticks, snowshoes, household vessels and utensils and, in some cases, canoe-making. During the war years, these crafts were carried on by the handicapped and the aged in the community. The younger women, who had the responsibilities connected with the household and the farm, had little time to pursue the quill and bead work, so highly prized in England. The artistic Elsie was interested in this work and was eager to learn the many techniques of embroidery, weaving, appliqué, wrapping and twisting of quills.

The temporary quarters provided for Elsie and John in the council house placed them at the heart of the Reserve activity, inasmuch as most of the public buildings were located there—the church, the school, the library, the store, as well as the buildings which housed engines, machinery, and equipment.

Saint Anne's Church, the most impressive edifice on the island was located across the road from the council house. John recalled the first Mass was celebrated there when he was just seven-and-a-half years old. He had made his first Communion in that church, he was confirmed there, served as an altar boy, sang in the choir and played the organ for many years.

The original log chapel built at the beginning of the nineteenth century by the Indians had been replaced in 1842 by a new chapel. When Lennox Island was purchased by the Aborigines' Protection Society of London, the trustees appointed for the management of the Reserve gave the Indians a piece of land designated on the map as chapel land. It consisted of five acres of farm land and five acres of woodland. The products from the land were to be sold and the money placed in a savings bank in Charlottetown to be used for building a new church. This church, unfortunately, was destroyed by fire.

According to the elders, John's father (John Thomas Sark) and his uncle (Anthony Mitchell) traversed the entire province of Prince Edward Island soliciting funds for a new church—one went east, the other west. Fifteen hundred dollars had already accumulated in the church fund. The present church was erected in 1895 and a wire and board fence was built around the chapel and burial ground. The steeple from the old church, mounted with a cross, was placed in the cemetery. At the same time a number of maple and birch trees were planted. In 1904 the parochial house was built under the supervision of Rev. John A. McDonald at a cost of $600. The Indians loved Father John A. and were amused when he referred to the glebe house as his wigwam. The bell in the tower of the church was donated later by men of the Holy Name Society. A significant fixture, the bell tolled to announce any event of importance to the resident community. When the bell sounded, the community assembled.

There were many mementoes of early days on Lennox Island. The wooden crucifix resting on the altar, for example, was said to have been carved by a resident some two hundred years before. This particular crucifix was one of six large crucifixes carried by elders of the church during religious processions when there was no resident priest. Traditionally, the elders would lead the people in prayer. When an elder died one of the six younger people would be appointed to take his place in the processional. The young person's position would be filled through elections from the Indian assembly.

On the wall near the altar there was an old pair of handmade wooden crutches, said to have been about one hundred and fifty years old. Apparently, these crutches belonged to an Indian who was afflicted with tuberculosis of the spine. In his whole life he had never been able to walk without crutches. However, while attending Holy Mass one St. Anne's Sunday, he prayed for the use of his legs. Later, as he stood up to receive Holy Communion, he walked to the altar, leaving his crutches on the seat.

Elsie was fascinated by this story and the many miraculous cures associated with Saint Anne which she heard on Lennox Island. In time, she herself came to understand and appreciate the spiritual significance of the mission of St. Anne in the life of the Micmac community. In July, she would have occasion to see for herself how their so-called grandmother St. Anne became the focal point of the Micmac cultural activities.

The schoolhouse, too, was of interest to Elsie. In addition to receiving his elementary schooling and preparation for St. Dunstan's College here, John had been the schoolteacher for five years prior to the war. Since the outbreak of war, his brother Jacob had taken over and was proving his dedication to elementary education. The school was built in 1898, replacing the original one which had been erected and furnished by the Indian Branch of the federal Department of the Interior in 1875.

A frame building, twenty-six feet by twenty, with thirteen posts on a red sandstone foundation, was supposed to accommodate fifty pupils. Although there were more school age children than that on the Island, the number on the school register was about 45. John recalled having about 42 attending at one time; Jacob had 41 at the present time. The one classroom, with a cloakroom at the entrance, extended the full width of the building. Windows on each side of the classroom gave adequate lighting, and heat was provided by a large wood stove. It was warm and comfortable in winter. According to John, it was altogether too small for the number of children present. He even had to store wood in the cloakroom during the winter.

The school was furnished with old-fashioned wooden desks, arranged in two rows along the length of the room. The desks were in good repair. There was a janitor who swept the school every day and had it scrubbed frequently. John recalled how he had had the place fumigated his first year of teaching because of an epidemic of smallpox the preceding year. When he left the school in 1914, four years earlier, it was fairly well supplied with books, slates, paper and maps. He had supplemented the small three by six-foot blackboard with a hyloplate one, sixteen by four feet. There were three large wall maps—the world, the Dominion of Canada, and Prince Edward Island. To brighten up the barren classroom, he had procured framed pictures and ordered roller blinds for the windows. He had left a good supply of Goggins' *New Elementary Grammar* texts and the PEI edition of the *New Canadian Geography*. A cupboard had not been provided in the school for supplies, but the teacher had a large desk where all supplies not in use could be locked up.

The school was centrally located and seemed to be in good condition. It compared favorably, as far as Elsie could judge from exterior appearances, with other rural school buildings on Prince Edward Island. All the children lived within easy distance of the school, the farthest away being one and a half miles. Although it was situated on an acre of land, the one shortcoming was insufficient space for the children to play games because a large part of the playground was covered with spruce. He was successful in having bushes cleared and the land levelled, but the department was not prepared to go to the expense of fencing the land.

John smiled as he recalled the visit of J.D. Sutherland from Ottawa during his first year of teaching. The visitor told him to use English only and to have the children speak it at all times. Then he challenged him to make Lennox Island Indian Day School one of the best Indian schools in the Maritime provinces. John felt he had succeeded in doing that. The Indian Superintendent, J.O. Arsenault, had tried to discredit him on the grounds he was too strict with the children. However, consistent reports of school inspectors and the results of pupil examinations bore silent witness to his success as a teacher. According to the report of the Indian Agent during his last year of teaching (1914), the public school inspector who visited the school "declared that he found it in a high state of efficiency and in many respects superior to several schools attended by white children."[4]

As the perennial problem was school attendance, he had recommended that a truant officer be appointed. That had helped for a while. His brother Jacob found it equally difficult to have all the children attend regularly. Part of the problem originated in the usual spring migration after the crops were sown. Many of the families would leave the Reserve for places in the vicinity of the railroad stations, where they would have access to raw materials and markets for their products. Here they would pitch tents and return only for St. Anne's Day on July 26. After a week's stay, they would be away again for two or three months and return for the winter season. In the cold winter months, poverty operated to prevent children from attending school. This the Indian Agent would attempt to obviate by issuing footgear and clothing. Many who might attend at this particular time were gathering wood for themselves or for some of the women whose men had gone to the front.

Fundamentally, however, the problem was a socio-political one. Those who kept their children out of school or sent their children to white schools on the mainland did so because the teacher was the son of Chief John Thomas Sark. The story of the Sark dynasty and the rivalry between two factions living side by side on this tiny Reserve was another surprise for Elsie. Things were relatively quiet now that the men were at the war. One post-war election for Chief of the Band would shed some light on this lengthy conflict.

The public hall, constructed during John's second year of teaching, was a welcome addition to the local community. It was fifty by twenty-five feet with an arched ceiling finished in natural wood. The walls were plaster, and the building had a good stage and a flagpole. It was furnished with hardwood chairs, and supplied with a stove and lamps. Apart from the furniture, the total cost was about $1,000. It was meant to serve as a cultural or social centre, for school and community concerts, for the instruction of the girls in the art of making moccasins and bead-work, and as a library. For John, the hall was another example of the benevolence of the British to the Micmacs of Prince Edward Island. It was named the Lady Wood Library after its donor, Lady Louisa Augusta Wood.

Louisa Augusta was a daughter of Lieutenant-Governor Edmund Fanning, who during his term of office (1786-1805) on Prince Edward Island acquired land amounting to 2,513 acres, which he left to his daughters. Louisa Augusta later married Colonel Wood of the British army and went to England. In her will, dated May 5, 1870—the same year Lennox Island had been purchased for the Micmac Indians—she directed that the land in Township 67 in Queens County be sold and one half of the proceeds be set aside for the benefit of the Indians. Inexplicably the will was lost until

1910, when the 40-year old parchment was discovered in the attic of the court house in Charlottetown. A trust had been created, but it had never been administered. In the meantime the government had sold the land and had issued government deeds to the new owners. An act was passed "to provide compensation to the trustees of the estate of Dame Louisa Augusta Wood for certain lands on Township No. 67 sold by the Commissioner of public lands." The preamble recited the pertinent facts and by agreement with the trustees, the act authorized the payment of the sum of $8,500 to the trustees as the share of the fund to be allotted for the benefit of the Indians. An annual income of approximately $800 from the Lady Wood estate has been used for the benefit of the Indians, providing the funds for the new community centre.[5]

The grocery store had been in operation for five years, in 1918. It was initiated by an enterprising young native by the name of Lemuel Bernard and he was doing a good business providing a great convenience to the locals. Nearly all the supplies given to the destitute Indians from the relief funds, especially during the winter months, were furnished by Mr. Bernard. The same year that the store opened, the federal government established a post office on the Reserve, and John's father was appointed the first postmaster.

As Elsie moved through the community, and particularly when she visited Micmac families in their homes, she became more and more aware of the fact that she was in the midst of a people with whom she would have little common ground, linguistically or culturally.[6] Here was a happy, carefree, community-oriented people, living close to nature, speaking their native language. They were genuinely loyal to one another, and apparently shared everything they had, especially with those in need. They prized their children and permitted them to do as they pleased. The poverty was appalling; yet, families which were actually destitute seemed well satisfied that basic food and clothing were being provided by the Indian Agent. Theirs was a mentality based on the adage "live and let live," a life-style diametrically opposed to everything Elsie had ever experienced.

Lennox Island was definitely not the setting for the life she envisaged in Canada! However, she had crossed the Atlantic to make John well; his recovery remained her top priority. For the time being, therefore, she would repress her own preferences and focus her energies on restoring John's health, even if it meant settling temporarily on Lennox Island.

7 | Convalescent on the Reserve

On April 18, 1918, just three weeks after the young couple's arrival on Lennox Island, John was notified of his posting to the Hospital Section, Halifax No. 6 District Depot. By this time Elsie was familiar with the Reserve and had found companionship in her sister-in-law, so she was prepared to remain behind when John left for Nova Scotia. Besides, she had a host of things to do, not the least of which was the chore of writing home.

She knew her family would be anxious to hear from her. They would want to know about her trip across the Atlantic, how she was, the state of John's health, and where she was located. She was aware of the fact that her father's sixty-fourth birthday had come and gone already. She would write first to her mother; the letter could be shared with her father and two sisters. She would need to write separate letters to her three brothers who were somewhere on the battlefields of Europe. Then, she had promised to write to her friend Margaret Dunne and to her sister-in-law living in Quebec.

Here she was, now, three thousand miles from the people she had known and loved all her life. How she had romanticised about her life with John in Canada. Now, the reality! She would not mention to her family and friends that she would be living temporarily in a room above the Indian Band Office in the council house, devoid of such basic necessities as running water and toilet facilities. Why worry them with her personal problem when their very lives were in constant peril in war-torn England. She would maintain a stiff upper lip. She would do what her mother had admonished her to do—"Grin and bear it."

As it happened, John's absence from home was short-lived. On May 4, sixteen days after he went to Halifax, he was given a temporary discharge certificate on the grounds of "being medically unfit for further service." An elated John returned with haste to Lennox Island to begin the designated period of recuperation. His discharge from the armed forces was formally confirmed on June 1, 1918. That same day John took possession of the twenty-five acres of land he owned on Lennox Island and began to make plans for a more comfortable home on the Reserve. By this time Elsie had made it clear that she had no intention of establishing roots there, but agreed it was an ideal place for her husband to convalesce. The understanding was that as soon as John was strong enough to work on the railway, they would move to Moncton, New Brunswick. Her two brothers had succeeded in making good lives for themselves and their families in Quebec and Ontario; such a move could be the first step in the achievement of a similar future.

John's property was located about a quarter of a mile from his father's house, just five hundred feet from his brother Jacob's home. It was bounded on the north by the Gull Point Road, on the south by the shoreline, on the east by a bog, and on the west by the church farmland. Plans for a frame wooden house thirty-five by twenty-five by ten feet were quickly drawn up and arrangements were made for the digging of a thirty-foot well. Twenty acres of property were deemed fit for cultivation. Elsie felt that small-scale farming would be a healthy pastime for her husband. He required lots of fresh air; there would be opportunities for light outdoor chores. Moreover, home-grown garden vegetables and fruit, as well as plenty of cow's milk would provide the essentials of his diet. Then, too, a flower garden was a must for anyone with English roots. During the month of June, a beginning was made. John supervised the clearing of ten acres of land and the construction of their new home; Elsie was hired as a full-time nurse ministering to a sick family in the white neighbourhood of Port Hill on the mainland. The income for her services, small though it was, was a welcome supplement to John's army pension.

Mrs. George Clow (née Richards) recalls with gratitude the nurse who cared for her and nursed her back to health when she was stricken with pneumonia in 1918.[1] "When I was a child," she said, "Mrs. Sark seemed so tall. I remember she was awfully nice to me when I was ill." Then the seventy-seven year old woman reminisced that Elsie stayed with them for a month while the house was being built on Lennox Island.

> From our house we could hear the hammering of nails from across the channel. We knew when the men were working on Mrs. Sark's home.
>
> My sister and I had pneumonia: I was five years old; my sister was fifteen. I remember Mom saying that Carrie would still be living if Mrs. Sark had been with us earlier. The previous nurse opened all the windows.
>
> When my sister Bertha was born on July 2, 1918, Mrs. John Sark was midwife. She was also Bert's godmother and every year she would send her godchild a twenty-five cent note for her birthday. She did that up until the time Bert was married.
>
> Every woman in Grand River spoke highly of her and of the good she did in that community...When I visited her some thirty years ago, in the fifties, she was living by herself on Lennox Island. She was a marvelous woman.

On June 29, while Elsie was still living with the Richards family, John was summoned to the Dalton Sanatorium where the certificate of discharge was formally signed in the presence of Dr. William D. Garrison. Elsie's services were required by the Richards family for another three weeks. When she did return to Lennox Island the big cultural event of the year was at hand—St. Anne's Day.

Preparations for the pre-eminent Micmac holiday began well in advance.[2] In collaboration with Indian Agent Father John A. McDonald, Chief John T. Sark drew up the agenda for the festivities which were a unique combination of religious rites and tribal customs. Men and women seemed to know exactly what were their respective roles. The men prepared the path from the wharf to the church with trees and shrubs gathered from "up the Cove"; they erected an outdoor altar for Sunday Mass; and they set up the community hall for the midday meal and also built temporary booths for canteens and displays of handicrafts. The women assumed responsibility for cleaning the interior of the church, laundering the linen and decorating the altar with flowers from the neighbourhood. They set up a grotto around the huge statue of their patroness St. Anne and they prepared the food for the noon meal. Long-time friends from the white communities on the mainland were helpful this particular year because of the number of able-bodied Micmac men in the armed services.

Although St. Anne's Sunday itself was the highlight of the festivities, the Indians began to arrive at the St. Anne Mission three days in advance and remained for at least a week. Among the approximately three hundred arrivals were those who had left the Reserve temporarily to sell their wares, those from the other three Reserves on Prince Edward Island—Morell, Scotchfort, Rocky Point—and those who had moved to other provinces, particularly Nova Scotia and New Brunswick.

Elsie was deeply moved as she watched what seemed to be a procession of canoes and dories cross the channel and as she heard the chant of Indian hymns as the Micmacs neared the wharf. She was spellbound watching the natives make their way from the beach to the church and to the shrine of St. Anne, many of them crawling on their hands and knees. This was the time for reconciliation and healing, and they were confident St. Anne would heal their physical and spiritual infirmities.

St. Anne's Sunday, Elsie learned, was not only a cultural event for the Micmac Indians; crowds of tourists, pilgrims and picnickers were attracted to the tiny island, where they joined the native people in both worship and festivity. They came by car, by boat and by team. Motorists were advised by Island newspapers to come early as the road via Northam and Port Hill would be closed between 9 a.m. and 1 p.m. From the Port Hill wharf they were shuttled by boat across the channel. Many admitted they were terrified because so many people were packed into the little boats, but they were assured there was nothing to fear as long as the natives were ferrying the boats. The crowd peaked by mid-afternoon. Elsie noted there were more whites than Indians. This was the first occasion since she left home that she had seen so many people gathered in one place.

The highlight of the Sunday morning activities was the celebration of Mass at ten o'clock. Since the weather was fine, this service was conducted outdoors to accommodate the large number assembled for worship. The outdoor altar was decorated with flowers from the roadside and local gardens; candles and incense were in readiness. The pastoral setting—the red earth, green grass, the cloudless sky and the deep blue water—made a perfect background for the service.

This year, Father John A. McDonald was the principal celebrant of the Mass. Servers were all Indian children. The musical part of the service was supplied by the Micmacs, in Latin, and in the Micmac language. After the Communion Service, Chief Sark, clad in full Indian regalia, welcomed the congregation to the various events scheduled for the remainder of the day. The liturgical celebration, he reminded them, would conclude with Vespers and Benediction.

Throughout the day, Elsie noted, the pilgrims made their way to the shrine of St. Anne in the chapel. The centrality of their patroness in the festivities was reflected in the prominence given to the immense statue. Unpretentious flowers hand-picked from open fields and home gardens were artistically arranged around the grotto. The statue of St. Anne, decked with gold crown and gold embroidered olive-green mantle over a salmon coloured gown was encased within a bower of green leaves. It made a spectacular scene. Elsie must have been touched by the faith of the assembly—Micmac and white—as they approached the shrine, made the sign of the cross, knelt in silent prayer for a few seconds, deposited their offerings, reverently kissed the feet of the statue which symbolized so much, and humbly withdrew.

Elsie was not familiar with this second-century Christian tradition of honouring St. Anne as the mother of Mary and the grandmother of Jesus. This is devotion to what the Indians called Niskan's mother. There was no mention of it in her Book of Common Prayer and there was no hymn to St. Anne listed in her favourite Church of England hymnal. She was impressed by the artist's rendition of Mary, dressed in blue, in the arms of Anne who looked fondly down upon her daughter. She must have been moved by the congregational participation in the traditional prayers and hymns, especially the zest with which all present joined in the refrain to the closing hymn:

O, good Saint Anne
We call on thy name
Thy praises loud
Thy children proclaim.

Her own religious feelings were no doubt in tune with those of the pilgrims. It was the occasion to implore "good St. Anne" to intercede for her husband's health, for her family's safety during the war, and for the two-month-old child in her womb.

Elsie could not fail to note the social and economic significance of this festival. An open invitation was extended to everyone through the news media to join in the celebration. It was obvious from the turnout that for Islanders at large, this was an annual event. From the church and the shrine, the people wandered freely about the island's roads, lanes and shore or sat to chat with friends and acquaintances. Some came in real picnic style with lunches prepared; others depended on the canteens and community hall for refreshments. Some gathered in the games area to watch the children display their athletic prowess.

This year they were particularly proud of Barney Francis from Indian River, who was champion runner in the Atlantic marathon. Others gathered in the amusement area where the children clad in their Sunday best were enjoying the circus-like attractions. It was a day for the Indian people to manifest their own culture: many were dressed in native costumes, and some participated in native dancing, while others took advantage of the opportunity to display and sell authentic Indian handicrafts. All in all, it was a great day for the Indians and the whites alike. For Elsie, it must have been a veritable morale builder. In one day she had met more white people than in the previous four months. It was a cultural event to which she and her husband whole-heartedly committed their time and talents in the years to come.

The election of chief was one business item associated with "mission week" celebrations which was dreaded by the women. According to the Indian Act, elections were to take place every three years. It was the occasion for political factions to surface in the course of which loyalties were tested. This, in turn, gave rise to drinking, fighting and all sorts of unpleasantness. In 1915, when most of the young men were overseas, Chief Sark suggested that a formal election not be held, but it was overruled. In the election that ensued John Thomas Sark had a clear majority of the vote over contestant Isaac Peters his half-brother. He received 75 percent of the vote cast. Now, three years later, most of the men were still at the front. Since there were no further nominations for the position, John T. Sark was declared elected by acclamation for another term of three years. In the absence of the usual drinking and brawling connected with elections, the festivities this year were much quieter than usual. The natives were so preoccupied and emotionally concerned with the safe return of their menfolk that they were not disposed to dispute about relatively unimportant matters. They would leave the management of the Band to Chief Sark and Father John A.

Much to Elsie's surprise, the summer of 1918 passed quickly. Lennox Island proved to be more than a refuge and a gathering place for the Micmac Indians; it was a veritable summer resort where the salt water of Malpeque Bay and the bright sunshine combined to produce an atmosphere conducive to peaceful and healthy living. Elsie felt in her own country this setting would be a vacation haven for English folk of noble heritage. Supervising the details of their home, along with the harvesting and preserving of garden crops, kept Elsie gainfully occupied. There were optimistic reports that the war would soon be over, with a sure victory for Britain and her allies. Then came the tragic news that Private Louis Toney, the Chief's stepson, was killed in action.

Despite the fact that under the Military Service Act, Indians in Canada were exempt from service, Prince Edward Island had an exceptionally high enlistment record in the First World War. For John Sark, there was good reason to defend the principles for which England stood; for others, it was a duty to help an ally of the Micmac Nation against its enemies; for most, it was a job with a salary. Besides, joining the army was perceived as the thing to do; most young men were eager to join and hoped that they would pass the acceptance test. The thirty-six Micmac volunteers in the khaki from Prince Edward Island "earned the highest praise for their exceptionally gallant conduct in action and particularly distinguished themselves in the great battle of Amiens."[3]

Seven of the community were killed in action, many of the remaining twenty-nine were wounded, and some suffered from asphyxiating gas. Elsie had grown fond of the women on the Reserve and hoped to be able to alleviate some of the pain for families whose men were suffered from the afflictions of gas poisoning.

Just one month after the armistice was signed while the residents were awaiting the return of their loved ones, the Reserve was saddened once again by the death of 20-year-old Nannet Toney, brother of Louis. Elsie sympathized with her mother-in-law while she gave thanks to God that her three brothers had come through the ordeal of war unscathed. Later she learned that her brother Harry had been in Kingston, Ontario, at that very time (just one month after the armistice was signed) going through the process of demobilization. He, who had introduced her to John Sark in the first place, made no effort to contact her or to inquire about her invalid husband. This, she knew, was typically English behaviour. She couldn't fail to note how sharply it contrasted with the Micmac ethos.

The long-awaited arrival of her first child came on the tenth of February, 1919, when Elsie gave birth to a baby girl. Three weeks later on March 2, 1919, their daughter was baptized by Reverend John A. McDonald in the Mission Chapel of Saint Anne on Lennox Island. She was given the names of Margaret Martha for her grandmothers Margaret Thornton Sark and Martha Ellis Houghton. Sponsors for the baby were John's brother-in-law John LaBobe and his niece Mary Agnes Mitchell, who was a school teacher at Rocky Point Indian Day School at the time. A few weeks later there was more good news for Elsie: the lesion on John's lung had healed and he was now able to return to the work force. She had taken him from Dalton Sanatorium to make him well, and she did! She had accepted the challenge and just one year after her arrival in Canada the first stage of her mission was accomplished. She was now in a position to move off the Reserve, to make a new beginning elsewhere in Canada.

8 | Volunteer Community-Worker

Before John mailed his application to the Canadian National Railway Office in Moncton, the Indian Agent prevailed upon him to remain on the Reserve. Father John A., a great friend of the Sark family, made frequent house calls to Elsie and John's home. He had been urging John not to leave Lennox Island, giving him plenty of reasons to remain on the Reserve. For one thing, Father reminded him, although he no longer had a tubercular lung, his heart was still somewhat enlarged; work on the railroad would be very strenuous. Furthermore, he and his wife had made an exceptionally good head start on the Reserve. They had invested a great deal of money, time and energy on their house and farm; it would be foolhardy for them to divest themselves of their assets at this stage of their young lives. Land on the Reserve could only be sold to another Indian, therefore there would be relatively little income in return for the property. Furthermore, there were many ways that he and his wife could influence the well-being of the Micmac people on the Reserve. Elsie was already doing a deal of good work among the women and children in the T.B.-ridden community, and it was no secret that John had been categorized by school inspectors as a born teacher. Certainly there was no one in the province with his expertise in Micmac, French and English.

John pondered the arguments confronting him and found himself in a real quandary. On the one hand, he did not want to disappoint Father John A., who had been so good to him over the years; on the other hand, he had promised Elsie that they would move off the Reserve when his health was restored. He would leave the decision to her. "I was all for going," she said, "but Father John coaxed me too." She was being asked to stay, not for the sake of her husband, but for the sake of his people and the church. This was a challenge for which she was not prepared, a challenge which would require an altogether different kind of response, one with far-reaching consequences. "Father John A. was a very good friend," she said, "so, in the end, we stayed."[1]

There was never any question as to how John would provide for his family. The Indian Agent had already seen to that. He had talked with Jacob regarding the teaching position at the school. Prior to the war, John had taught there for five years. Now Jacob was willing to resign his post as schoolteacher, in favour of his brother, providing John consented to remain on the Reserve. Actually, Jacob's teaching services were being requested by Chief Augustine of Big Cove, New Brunswick, and it was well-known that Jacob was interested in the Chief's daughter.

So, on April 1, 1919, on the first day of the new fiscal year, Jacob Sark resigned as teacher of the Lennox Island Indian Day School, and the following week, on April 8, John J. was recommended to the department as the best qualified person for the now vacant teaching post. One week later, the Department of Indian Affairs approved the recommendation. The understanding was that John J. would be paid the same salary as his brother, namely $400. Added to that, of course, was the supplement of $150. With John's army pension and a potential small farm, the judicious Elsie was satisfied that they would have no difficulty financially.

Having committed herself to live on the Reserve, for Elsie there was no turning back. Now that John was schoolteacher, she would make an extra effort to become involved in local community affairs. Ever since she worked for the Richards family at the Port Hill Corner, her services were in great demand "on the mainland"; however, she had observed the health problems on the Reserve and resolved to be of more assistance closer to home. She had come to admire the women on the Reserve, who were energetic and industrious, and there was much she could learn from them, especially about child-rearing, handicrafts and cooking. But, to be effective, she realized she would need to be fully accepted. Religion was highly valued in this community, so confirmation in the Catholic faith would have to be a priority. Accordingly, she joined her sister-in-law Elizabeth Mitchell for further instructions in the faith and by mid-June was ready to receive the Sacrament of Confirmation.

Sunday, June 15, 1919, was a red-letter day on the Reserve, bringing the Bishop of Charlottetown, Henry J. O'Leary, on a pastoral visit and to administer the Sacrament of Confirmation. The solemn entry of the bishop as he was received by Chief Sark and the whole Micmac tribe reminded Elsie of her own reception a year before. On this occasion, they were privileged to have a missionary priest, Father Pacifique, lead them in Vespers and Benediction.[2] The following morning Elsie was confirmed in the Catholic faith by the bishop, along with twenty-three others—there were twelve males and twelve females. Sponsors were John's father and stepmother—Chief John T. Sark and Lady Annie May (Toney) Sark.

Elsie was pleased that the "neo-confirmati" were given the "total abstinence pledge." While John was not intemperate, he was not a total abstainer. She had been told that poverty and drunkenness were the main impediments to progress on the Reserve and she was beginning to see the effects of liquor on the morale, especially the women. The local Temperance Society, which had been active since the mid-nineteenth century, was doing good work. She was glad to know that leadership was available in this regard. The Bishop commended the community on the fact that "in the whole history of the tribe, not one had lost the faith." He further commended them on their patriotism in the recent war. The final portion of the ceremony took place outdoors in the cemetery where His Excellency performed the service of Absolution of the Dead.

Elsie was impressed by the simple faith of all who had participated in the confirmation services. In a month's time, she knew, they would go all out once again to celebrate the feast of St. Anne. The rites and devotions of the Catholic Church appealed to her. She would join the pilgrims thanking St. Anne for the many graces and blessings of the past year and seek her assistance in the years ahead.

Now, as her commitment to living on the Reserve was being forged, she would be more closely in touch with the unusual circumstances of her new life. As time passed, the conflict between her own values and the Micmac ethos understandably set her at odds with members of the community. But the strength of her religious conviction, her genuine interest in the Reserve, and her unflagging devotion to service in the community whenever needed carried her through the difficult times.

True to her nature and disposition, Elsie lost no time helping John make plans for their family's future. Father John A. had urged them to take advantage of the loans available through the Soldier Settlement Act to improve their property; he would vouch for the loan. True, they already had the essentials—a house which was nearly finished, and a horse which provided transportation. However, since they planned to stay, she felt they ought to have their own milk cow and a barn. Besides, the woven wire fence they had put around their ten acres of cultivated land had not yet been paid for. John admired his wife's earnestness, enthusiasm and energy and began the paperwork on negotiations in July for a barn ($300), a cow ($75), and fencing ($35). His application was endorsed by the Indian Agent in August.

The young couple then applied for insurance against fire or damage by fire or lightning through the Soldier Settlement Act. The indenture was made on September 30 with the understanding it would be interest-free for two years and payment on interest and principal would begin at the end of three years. In the meantime, Elsie had purchased a Jersey cow from Annie May Sark; the following spring they would begin work on the barn. For the time being, John concentrated his energies on improving the physical and academic status of the local school, while she focused her energies on the home, farm and family.

Events of the next five years, from 1919 to 1924, set the stage for their future in the community. The far-reaching effects of seemingly insignificant acts cannot be foreseen, and putting together a new life was, for Elsie and John Sark, a priority. And September 10, 1920 was a time to rejoice, for Elsie, without the assistance of a medical doctor, gave birth to a baby boy. The mother's instinct alerted her to the fact that this child was not hers for long. For Elsie, being born is not all there is to life, so arrangements were made to have the child baptized on the very day of his birth. John Reuben was named for his father and grandfather Sark and for his maternal great-grandfather Ellis. That same year there was more good news for the growing family; John was granted an increase in his school salary!

The period of rejoicing for the young family, however, was short-lived. The next year, 1921 was a year to weep. On April 8, 1921 Elsie received word of the sudden death of her father at Cliffe Cottage, Dover. Literally speaking, Charles Houghton had died with his boots on, the day following his sixty-seventh birthday. As much as Elsie would have liked to have been present to comfort her mother and to mourn with her sister Nellie, she knew in her heart that a trip to Dover was out of the question. There was no way her husband could cope single-handedly with the school, the farm and two young children. Marto, as John loved to call his daughter, was just two years of age, and John Reuben was in delicate health. When, less than three months later on July 4, 1921, the nine-month-old John Reuben was laid to rest in the cemetery of St. Anne's Mission Church, Elsie knew she had made the right decision.

While the young mother was still mourning the loss of her first-born son, another letter edged in black reached her from Dover. Elsie was beside herself. Nellie had kept her abreast of the family events following their father's death—the move to Tower Hamlets, her mother's failing health and eventual transfer to the hospital on Union Road—but she was not emotionally ready to face the news of her mother's death, the third death in seven months. Ever since John Reuben's death, friends had been suggesting that she take a trip to Dover. Money was no obstacle, to be sure. The Anglican minister at Port Hill had offered to pay her fare to England. Father John A., not to be outdone, informed her that he would finance her trip should she decide to go.

Elsie, however, valiantly pulled herself together and decided that rather than go away, she would put herself in the service of others. It so happened her work was cut out for her; it was a time for service! In 1919, when there was an epidemic of influenza in Canada, Lennox Island had been fortunate; there were only three deaths on the Reserve. During the next five years, however, close to fifty residents in the small community died, more than one-fifth of these deaths resulted from T.B.

After the war the Red Cross Society had launched a peace-time program, and from 1920 to 1924 the society had carried the burden of public health on Prince Edward Island. Nevertheless, its services at this time did not extend to this remote area. On May 1, 1924, Miss Margaret Grier, assistant-secretary of the Canadian Anti-Tuber-culosis Association reported in the *Charlottetown Guardian* that Prince Edward Island was the only province in Canada which was doing virtually nothing in the field of preventive work against T.B., and that as a province it had the highest death rate from the disease.

Seven more years elapsed before a Department of Public Health was established in the province. The Lennox Island Reserve was under the federal health authority, but service was poor. By all accounts, during the twenties, Mrs. Sark was the only nurse servicing the area and she was tireless in her efforts to bring relief to the sick and dying. As nurse and community worker, she gained the respect and admiration of all to whom she ministered.

Meanwhile, just two years after John Reuben's death, on July 5, 1923, with the assistance of Dr. J.A. Stewart of Tyne Valley she gave birth to a second daughter. This child was baptized Ellen Rebecca, for her aunt Ellen Houghton (soon to be Mrs. Wilfred Taylor) and for her maternal great grandmother Rebecca Ellis. In the interim between the birth of her two daughters (1919-1923), Elsie had been midwife to more than half the births on the Reserve. According to the Roadmasters Registry Record, she was "doctor in attendance" many times over. During that same three-year period and, indeed, for the next three years, Rebecca Sark was the only child on the Reserve who was welcomed into this world by a medical doctor!

Her assiduity and perseverance also paid off on the home front. At the close of their first five years on Lennox Island, the Indian Agent reported to the Soldier Settlement authorities that the Sark estate was flourishing. According to the memorandum, the house had a concrete foundation, was well furnished and in good repair; the barn and stable, too, were in good condition; the fifty chains of barbed-wire fence enclosing a part of the property was in good condition; in fact, the farm, in general—a large part of which was under hay and pasture—was in good condition. More specifically, under cultivation were one acre of wheat, one acre of oats, three-quarters of an acre of potatoes; and, in addition, there were fifteen acres of hay. Livestock consisted of two horses, two cows, two calves, thirty chickens and eleven young geese. Farm implements included a plough, a harrow, a truckwagon, a seeder. These were housed in a barn and were in good condition. Besides, they had on hand ten cords of summer wood.

The school report was no less positive, and it was no secret that Elsie was John's chief advisor when it came to the rules of health for the school and school children. Cleanliness was next to godliness! The school was scrubbed every two months. John was fortunate, too, in having the backing of Inspector R. Brewer Auld in his requests for such physical improvements as having the exterior of the schoolhouse whitewashed, the interior painted in bright colours, the leaky roof shingled. Heating was a real problem. In 1922 a globe heater stove replaced a badly cracked and dangerous one. Department approval was not given for a cement foundation, so, to prevent draughts during the cold winter months, the basement of the school was "banked" each fall. When efforts to obtain a coal shed were not successful, John reluctantly used the cloakroom for this purpose.

Academically the school had an excellent reputation during this same five-year period. Inspector Auld not only gave a good report on the standing of the school to the Indian Agent, but also publicised in the provincial newspapers that the Lennox Island Indian Day School was on a par with the white schools in the surrounding districts and, in some things, was above average. Evidence of the progress of the pupils in the various branches of study was carefully recorded at least twice a year, once prior to the Christmas holidays and again during the end of the school term. John used to invite outsiders—parents, trustees, the Indian Agent, the inspector and officials from the Department of Indian Affairs—to attend a performance in connection with announcing the results of examinations and the awarding of prizes. The program for December 1923 is typical:

Program
(1) Holy Mary Mother Mild
(a) English Catechism 1st Class
(b) English Catechism 2nd Class
(c) English Catechism 3rd Class
(a) Micmac Catechism 1st Class
(b) Micmac Catechism 2nd Class
(c) Micmac Catechism 3rd Class
(2) O Canada
Grammar
(3) It's Not the House That Makes the Home
5th Standard and Tables
3rd Standard and Tables
(4) We'll Never Let the Old Flag Fall
2nd Standard and Tables
1st Standard and Tables
(5) Maple Leaf Forever
Geography
(6) God Save the King

74

The contents suggest some mix of Micmac values and loyalties in with the English curriculum. The basic subjects examined—grammar, arithmetic, reading and geography—reflected the curriculum of the provincial schools. But this was a federal school, and as the Micmac were Roman Catholic, it is not surprising that the Micmac catechism was used. Comprised as it was of five parts, a catechism for children, principal truths of the faith, hope and prayer, sacraments, charity and commandments, and principal prayers, it could be adapted to the different levels of instruction.[3] Over and above the formal curriculum, loyalties to the Church, the crown, the country, and the tribe seem to have been transmitted indirectly through music and language.

John obviously was master in his own professional field. Not only did he use Micmac as a language of instruction, even after being admonished by federal authorities to use English only in the classroom and to insist the pupils use English at all times, but he took advantage of every opportunity for his pupils to show their proficiency in their native tongue. Micmac, he explained to the school inspectors, was the language used in the homes and was, therefore, a necessary vehicle through which concepts contained in the prescribed English textbooks could be conveyed.

Elsie gave her full support to John's educational endeavours. At the end of the program, she treated all present with candy, cake and peanuts. Her involvement did not go unnoticed. In the official report to the Department of Indian Affairs in 1924, she was personally mentioned for "her active interest in school concerts and other activities that make for progress."

Around this time when all seemed to be running smoothly on the home and school fronts, two incidents took place which resulted in strained relationships between the Sark family and a small sector of the Micmac community.

The first occurred in the fall of 1923 when a veteran, who had been gassed during the Great War, used abusive language to Mrs. Sark. Being the person she was, Elsie could not be silent. Accordingly, she reported Mr. Thaddy Knockwood to the appropriate authority. He was arrested and taken to Summerside where he was convicted and sentenced to a fee of ten dollars and costs. Mrs. Sark's action in regard to a veteran, a respected member of the community prior to the war, was repudiated by the Micmacs. In their opinion her behaviour was not only inappropriate, it was downright disloyal. Such conduct would not be tolerated on the Reserve; she would not be allowed to get away with it. To make matters worse, the excitement associated with the proceedings had an adverse effect on Mr. Knockwood's health and necessitated his being hospitalized, first in the Charlottetown Hospital and afterwards in Camp Hill Military Hospital in Halifax.

In the meantime, the peace-loving John, sensitive to anything that might upset his English wife, attempted to forestall further problems. To avoid a potential frame-up, he requested that the eighteen-year-old daughter of Mr. Knockwood not return to school. This was the opportune time for retaliation and John became the scapegoat.

In February 1924, letters of complaint were sent to Ottawa from Mr. Knockwood and the school trustees requesting that John J. Sark be replaced by a white teacher because of his "intemperate habits" and "cruelty to children." These were counteracted by letters from the Chief and parents of the school children who claimed it would be a great mistake to remove the teacher. According to their version, John J. Sark was painstaking toward the children; the rumour about his intemperance was false; and, the girl in question was unladylike and used abusive language in the presence of young children. The Department of Indian Affairs responded by directing the Indian Agent to look into the matter.

In the investigation, John J. Sark was able to convince the authorities that he acted in the best interests of the school and the students. "I have always tried," he wrote, "to treat the children alike and to be honest with all of them." He explained that the girl in question was beyond the compulsory school attendance age; that nothing further could be gained by her continued attendance which, at best, had been sporadic over the past thirteen years; and that the younger children needed the time that was being devoted to her individually. Mr. J.D. MacLean, Assistant Deputy and Secretary of Indian Affairs was satisfied. He wrote to the Indian Superintendent, Father John A., "Kindly inform the Indians that the Department has no intention of dispensing with the services of Mr. Sark, and that, instead of hindering him by trivial complaints, the Department expects that they will assist him in encouraging a regular attendance."

The two incidents were settled promptly and favourably for Elsie and John, but tensions in the community now had a definite target. Those who wished to, perceived a wrong-doing towards Thaddy Knockwood and his daughter.

Elsie's response to this was to distance herself from the scene of the conflict, and she took the two girls, Marto and Becky, on a trip to Montreal. There, in the company of her brother Jack and his wife Bess, she relaxed until hostilities subsided, while back home on the Reserve, John went quietly on with business as usual, his only diversion was drink. Constant harassment from family and friends was wearing him down. He knew only too well that his support of Elsie's perceived breach of loyalty to the tribe did not augur well for either of them. Sooner or later they would pay a price.

9 | The Politics of Mistrust

L ittle realizing how deeply she had offended the Micmac sensibility by reporting Thaddy Knockwood to the police, Elsie returned from Montreal refreshed in body and spirit. She figured that she had been driving herself too hard and readily acquiesced when her husband suggested she discontinue long hours of work on the land. Heretofore they had been dependent on the crops to supplement their earnings, so John applied and was successful in obtaining an increase in his school salary. Thanks to her good management, they were well off economically.

Now it was important for Elsie to restore her public image in the community. She felt that she had not really "lost face" in the eyes of the women on the Reserve, that she had actually gained their secret admiration by fearlessly standing up to Mr. Thaddy Knockwood. She assumed that they had not openly supported her out of fear and, therefore, she was sensitive to their feelings of shame and embarrassment. She prayed that God would help her bear her own hurt in silence so that others would not be burdened with guilt.

Nevertheless, for the time being she would mingle less among the people on the Reserve, curtail her volunteer health activities, while making it abundantly clear that she would be at their beck and call should her services be required. But strengthening her ties with the neighbouring white community on the mainland, was in fact one outcome this incident.

The gulf that separated the Reserve community from their white neighbours was far wider and deeper than the channel of water that lay between the island and the mainland. Elsie, however, a stranger in both places, had no difficulty making friends. Her daily visits to the markets in Port Hill and Tyne Valley and her Sunday visits to Saint Patrick's parish church in Grand River brought her in touch with people who became her lifelong friends. She would capitalize upon their friendship while attempting to regain the confidence of the native women. But she must have known that identification with the white establishment would be still another barrier to acceptance by the Micmac community.

Many of the elders of the area—Catholic and Protestant alike—recall with affection and admiration the English woman they met in the mid-twenties. Their reminiscences shed much light on Elsie as a person and her status in the white community.

The Browns were one of the few Roman Catholic families living in the Anglican village of Port Hill. Their daughter-in-law Jessie recalls visits by Mrs. Sark.

> I recall she came to the Brown household two or three times a week to visit, and stayed; it didn't matter who was there. Even in the winter she came across the ice with the nice little horse she had—that horse could almost talk—and a jaunting sleigh. One night I was wishing she would leave early because there was a really bad snowstorm. Around ten o'clock Harold went out and got on horseback and went ahead of her. He put her on the road leading to the wharf and returned home. Somehow, instead of going straight across, she got astray and spent the night in Henry Maynard's woods. She put a buffalo over the horse and another over herself and settled in the sleigh for a quiet night. When she arrived home in the morning her husband was lighting the stove; no questions were asked. She very rarely stayed away. He probably assumed she stayed at our place all night. I doubt if she told him.[1]

Another local woman who had high regard for Mrs. Sark, Mina Strongman, remembers that when Mrs. Sark came across to the Port Hill store and post office after visiting "her Catholic neighbour" she would come to see her too.

> I had a store at the Port Hill Corner for ten years. There was no store on Lennox Island at the time, so I got to know the Indians well.

79

I respected them all and I guess they me. When they were drinking they called me "Mom." I would put the run to them. They never got mad at me. The next day they would come back and admitted that I did right.

Mrs. Sark would come across from wharf to wharf, sometimes in her own boat, sometimes by ferry, and we had great chats in the store. I was her best friend on the mainland after the Browns. It was a pleasure to know her. She was not hard to know, easy to get acquainted with. She was like one of us. She came and talked her problems over, a wonderful person, what I call a nice down-to-earth woman. She had that nice way of an English woman and I love that.

I gathered she had a difficult time adjusting, but she did not find it hard once she got there, got settled, and got to know the people. She was a great worker with the other women and really enjoyed her life.[2]

Another secret admirer of Mrs. Sark was Marguerite Maynard. It was only after her marriage in 1927, when she came to live in the Maynard home (which was situated on the road leading to the Port Hill wharf) that she became personally acquainted with her. Her husband, Hatfield, remembered Mrs. Sark when she first came in 1918. She herself became very fond of Mrs. Sark, looked up to her for what she was and for what she did.

When we got a car, my husband often took Mrs. Sark to the train or bus. She was not shy about asking for a drive, not a bit! She was a fine looking woman. The first time I went to a funeral on Lennox Island (before I was married) she stood out—she was distinguished looking. She was dressed, I remember, in a blue suit. Even with a cotton dress, she looked dressy.

I admired her for coming here, not knowing a soul. I couldn't have done it! If she needed potatoes, she came and got them. She never wanted for the necessities in anything.

I never saw her angry or depressed. She was the same all the time. She never complained, never once. She came and stayed, delivered and clothed half the children on the Reserve. If anyone went to the Sark home, they were well-treated; she was always nice.[3]

Bessie MacNeil, whose son Roderick now runs the store at the Tyne Valley Corner, was brought up by her aunt Mrs. Sheldon Sharpe, in East Bideford, just across the water from Lennox Island. Bessie recalls Mrs. Sark's visits:

She always stayed for supper, even after my aunt died. She came to shop and stayed to visit. She was never short of money, never wanted for anything, always full and plenty.

I was a great friend of Becky and went to the Sark home on Lennox Island. I used to admire the way Mrs. Sark kept her home. She had a centre-piece of horses and chariot on the piano, something you would see in England. As a child, I thought it was pure gold! Her husband John was very good-looking, handsome in uniform; in fact, he was a striking-looking man.

She kept an English role; they know what is right and wrong. They are in command. At one time there was prejudice, but Mrs. Sark mixed with everyone, Indians and whites, Catholics and Protestants. She was a great church woman; her heart was in the Church. I never heard her say she was sorry she came to Lennox Island. The only thing I recall is when she went to England, she was glad to get back.[4]

Mrs. Howard MacKinnon (née Beatrice MacLellan) expressed great admiration for Elsie. She recalled the days when her father, Josie Joe MacLellan, directed the choir in Grant River.

My father brought them to the house after Mass—sometimes Mr. and Mrs. Sark, sometimes Mr. Sark and two of the children. He had a marvellous singing voice. He would sing and play the piano.

I knew Mrs. Sark personally and thought what it must have meant for her to come to such a primitive place after living in London, England. She was a grand person. On St. Anne's Day I went to her home and was impressed by what I saw, especially her kitchen range. It had a great big mirror on the warming oven which I greatly admired.[5]

For these interviewees and many other women on Prince Edward Island, this woman from Dover was the epitome of an English lady, descended, they thought, from royalty, and they treated her accordingly. She was respected by everyone, near and far, and referred to by the Victorian title "Mrs. Sark."

At home on the Reserve, she seems to have commanded a similar respect from her father-in-law. As Chief, his responsibilities brought him off the Reserve for long stretches of time, attending the meetings of the Grand Council and touring the lodges of his Micmac brethren throughout the Maritime provinces and Quebec. Even when on Prince Edward Island he was frequently tied up with meetings and other Band business, so he had Elsie sworn in as assistant post-mistress. Working for the federal government was a veritable morale booster for Elsie at this time. She saw this job as an opportunity to come into direct contact with most families on the Reserve. It was hoped that in the course of time, wounded friendships would be healed. The elders on the Reserve recall how as trappers, they would bring pelts to Mrs. Sark and she, in turn, would wrap, label, and mail them to such destinations as the Hudson Bay Company. Her son Ray tells the story of his mother's proficiency on the job. She could tell the trapper the exact amount of postage required without even placing it on the scales, simply by holding it in her hand! The Indians could not help but respect her skills and resourcefulness, although deep down, they resented who she was and what she had.

The year 1927 was hailed as the best of times by Elsie when, in February, she gave birth to a baby boy. Raymond James, as he was christened, was a blond-haired, fair-complexioned child, strongly resembling the Houghton side of the family. At the time he was born, eight-year-old Martha was well into her second year in the local school. Besides being her father's pride and joy, she was a great help to her mother, doing chores about the house and barn and, above all, amusing her three and one-half-year-old sister. By now the Sark family considered themselves an integral part of the Micmac community. They were economically better off than other families on the Reserve and, on this account, were an obvious target for envy and resentment.

As winter gave way to spring, everything had been going well for them. Then the rumour surfaced that Isaac Peters declared his intention to run for the position of Chief in the up-coming election. Inevitably, this meant that the community on the Reserve must divide itself in factions, and suffer the consequences.

Some initiative had been taken on the part of Chief Sark's friends and local politicians to have the now-aging chief declared a life-chief because of his long years of uninterrupted service; however, that was not possible as the system of life-chiefs had been discontinued some years before. Therefore, an election was scheduled, as usual, during the St. Anne's Day celebrations. This was to be the real test of love for Elsie.

Since she came to the Reserve in 1918, her father-in-law had been Chief of the Micmacs of Prince Edward Island, and Elsie had come to believe that chieftainship was part of the legacy of the Sarks. Now, after nine years in the family, she learned the saga of the Sark dynasty.[6] In the olden days, John told her, the position of chief was determined by heredity, handed down from father to son.

On October 25, 1859, George Dundas, Esq., Lieutenant and Commander-in-Chief of the Island, confirmed the appointment of John Sark as "Chief of the Indians of Prince Edward Island." That chief, his great grandfather, died in 1866, when his own father, John Thomas Sark was only seven years of age, so the position was given to the old chief's brother Louis Sark in 1868. The confusion regarding the Sark's family claim to the much-prized title of chief began after Louis Sark was deposed in 1869 on the grounds he drank too much. Peter Benard was elected to take his place on July 26 and remained chief until his death in 1877. Joseph Francis, a relative of John T. Sark's mother, was appointed to the position. According to the Sark version of this appointment, Joseph Francis was to be *acting* chief until John Thomas Sark became of age; Chief Francis, on the other hand, insisted that he was appointed life-chief. Whatever the truth of the matter may have been, twenty years later, in 1897, the Indians of Lennox Island (with the exception of a few families) lost confidence in Chief Francis and appointed John T. Sark—a lineal descendant of the original John Sark—as their new chief. John Thomas Sark was now thirty-eight years of age, was a resident of Lennox Island, was married and had a family of seven children. His appointment created bad feelings between the old chief's friends and those of the new chief, and gave rise to disputes and disagreements which have been simmering ever since.

When the Department of Indian Affairs learned from Superintendent J.O. Arsenault of the situation on Lennox Island, grave concern was expressed on the grounds that the election procedures had not been adhered to. The Indian Agent was directed to call a meeting for the purpose of rectifying the situation, with the understanding if a majority of the Indians wanted to have an election, the department would obtain the necessary permission from the Governor-General of Canada. A decision was made at a meeting on May 17, 1897, not to call an election. For the department, that meant Chief Francis was re-instated; for the Micmacs it meant John T. Sark was the new chief. This confusion was probably partly responsible for the discontinuity of life-chiefs by an Act of Parliament on May 16, 1899, and the authorization of the triennial system of election for all the Indian Bands in the older provinces. In 1900, Sark won the election for chief by a majority of nineteen votes, and was officially recognized on January 25, 1900. Because of unsafe weather conditions the declaration was not signed until April 27, 1900. The old chief, Francis, had not yet resigned from what he believed to have been a life appointment nor had he been deposed. Under these peculiar circumstances, the department permitted Joseph Francis to retain his title for life on the understanding that he would not be allowed to exercise the powers of office unless elected under the provisions of the act. He would be the last of the Micmacs to hold the title of life-chief.

John proudly reviewed the Sark record. With one exception since the year 1900, his father had consistently won each three-year election at the polls and held the post of Chief for the duration of each of the three-year terms, despite the efforts of his father's half-brother, Isaac Peters, and his followers to depose or defeat him. He made no secret of the fact that he anticipated tensions in the upcoming election. The tensions created would be deep-seated ones, stemming from the two factions which had existed side by side within the Band of Micmac Indians long before Elsie came to Canada. He vividly recalled the year his father had lost the election. It was the year he was about to assume his teaching career in the school. He was caught in the middle, so to speak, and experienced great frustration when families from one faction refused to send their children to school because the teacher belonged to the other faction—in this case, a Sark. John then reminded his wife that he personally had no interest in the position of chief; by nature he was the retiring type. He felt strongly, however, that despite the changes which had been effected at the turn of the century which abolished the concepts of "hereditary right to succession" and "life-chief," the chieftainship should remain on the Sark side of the family, not the Francis side. He made it clear to his wife that he would fight hard to this end each time election year came round.

Party politics, whether at the federal, provincial or local level, were of little interest to Elsie, mother of three young children. The election of 1927 was an eye-opener as she witnessed the power struggle within the Micmac clan. Despite the efforts of those responsible for the proceedings to forestall potential problems, there was much drinking and fighting. Eventually a riot broke out and conditions became such that the Indian Agent had to close the polls early. When the ballots were finally counted, she was taken aback to learn that Isaac Peters had a majority of the votes cast and was declared elected. This was the beginning of a three-year period of persecution for the Sarks and their supporters. Elsie had learned her lesson four years before; now that she was well-settled on the

Reserve and knew the lay of the land, she would not be intimidated, come what may.

No sooner was Peters sworn in as chief than he made two requests to Ottawa. The first was to dismiss John J. Sark as schoolteacher and to appoint a non-Indian in his place; the second was to dismiss his own half-brother, the ex-chief, as postmaster on the Reserve. In the inquisition that followed, the Postmaster General found no irregularity in the running of the post office, and the newly appointed school inspector not only gave the teacher a high rating on his performance in the classroom, but also recommended that he be given an increase in salary.[7]

One of the trustees, Constable John Francis, who had signed the petition to remove the teacher wrote privately to Ottawa. In his letter he pointed out that it would not be a good thing to change the teacher, that the new chief was pushing for the removal of John J. Sark "for spite." Moreover, of the twenty-three names signed to the petition for his removal, only seven lived on the Reserve and, of those seven, only three had children of school age. When the Indian Agent visited the school on February 1, 1928, he found that everything was "in the best of shape." He cited from reports of the past three inspectors, the most recent of which was written the preceding month:

> The pupils were examined in the various subjects. The results were the best I have ever obtained. Number of pupils present: 22. Schoolroom tidy and clean.
> W. Boulter, School Inspector

> I inspected this school today. I wish to complement Mr. Sark and his pupils on the neat, clean, tidy and attractive appearance of the school property. School building is in immediate need of repair or reshingling of the roof. Mr. Sark continues to do satisfactory work with the children. Politeness and courtesy are very noticeable. Writing and physical exercises are above the average.
> B. Brewer Auld, School Inspector

> I inspected the school today [Jan. 30, 1928] and very much pleased with the work so ably carried on by Mr. Sark. His pupils show they have been trained in manners and discipline. Their classwork is up to the standard of our schools and I must remark especially Spelling, Writing, Singing and Physical drill.
> Hilda W. Gillis, Inspector of School

Once again the authorities were satisfied that all was well in the post office and school and the matter was dropped. The new Chief resided seventy miles away so, in his absence, everything seemed to revert to normal. In actual fact, however, the ordeal was a devastating blow to the pride of John J. Sark. He began to drink more frequently.

It was no secret that John Sark enjoyed a drink. He drank socially with his friends as a teenager on the Reserve and again while he was in the army. It was a foregone conclusion that everyone on the Reserve drank at election time. There was always liquor of some sort (rum or brandy) in the Sark home which was shared with relatives and neighbours for medicinal purposes. John never drank when he was on duty; now he seemed to be drinking on weekends out of a sense of frustration. When sober, John was always the perfect gentleman; when drinking, he could be nasty. Friends of the Sark girls noted they were afraid of him when he was drinking. Elsie knew how to handle him on such occasions. When he would try to win her good graces by teasing her, her silence spoke louder than words. When the situation was beyond her power of endurance, she would simply cross over to the mainland and visit her friends. Never once did she divulge even to her best friends the reason for her temporary escape. She understood the root cause of her husband's problem and she was sympathetic. Any assault on his character or life-style he interpreted as an attack on his English wife whom he respected and loved, and with this he was unable to cope. Elsie knew it would take time and patience to help rebuild his own self-image. Just as she helped restore his physical health ten years before, so now she would do the same for his psychological health.

When the local school did not open on schedule in September, 1928, Elsie felt in her bones there would be trouble which would compound the drinking problem. She knew her husband was unable to do anything about the situation in which he found himself and she was sympathetic. She had faith that in the long run things would work out satisfactorily; she was determined to remain cool-headed. It so happened her brother Charles, who was with the Canadian Department of Militia, was in Charlottetown at the time, training the artillery. She hoped and prayed that the problem would be solved locally and quietly. After all, her pride, too, was at stake!

When John's long-time friend Mr. Sutherland of the school branch of the Department of Indian Affairs visited Lennox Island that month, he was informed that John Sark was in the hospital, having been injured in a drunken brawl, and that the school had not been opened after the summer holidays. The Indian Agent was asked for a report on the situation. Father John A. wrote as follows:

> John J. Sark, the teacher on Lennox Island, was in a brawl once to my knowledge during vacation. He was bitten by another Indian who was leader of the riot at the time of the election for chief. The bite did not amount to much at the time, but blood poisoning ensued. I had to send him to the hospital and after two operations and the amputation of one of his fingers, his hand was saved.
>
> The doctor expected to have him discharged from the hospital for the opening of the school, but it took longer than was expected. He was discharged cured on the 21st of Sept., returned to Lennox Island and opened the school on Monday the 24th inst. There was an attendance of 28 pupils—practically all the pupils at present on the Reserve.

Father John A. frankly admitted to the Deputy Superintendent that he favoured Sark and recommended that an outside official investigate the complaints against him as a teacher. He suggested that the Chief Inspector for the Maritime Province Indians, A.J. Boyd of River Bourgeois, N.S., might be a good choice. Father made it clear that he, personally, would like to set the matter at rest for all time!

The patience of J.D. MacLean, Assistant Deputy and Secretary of the department, was apparently wearing out. He wrote to the agent:

> The Department is of the opinion that the school will never operate at its maximum efficiency under Mr. Sark and that it would be in the best interests of the work if an outsider was appointed as teacher—one not interested in reserve cliques. It has, therefore, been decided that the services of John J. Sark be discontinued at the end of the present calendar year, December 31, next, and that a new teacher be engaged to begin duties early in January.

In the same communiqué the agent was asked to consult the provincial school inspector and to nominate a qualified teacher to commence duties at the beginning of the new year 1929. It would be preferable, the letter stated, to recruit a male teacher with at least a second-class license. It stipulated further:

In the event of a new teacher being obtained, please advise the Department if it would be necessary for him to occupy the residence on the reserve. If this house is required, due notice should be given to the present occupants to vacate. You might also report what repairs and furnishings would be required to make it comfortable for a new teacher.

The agent was annoyed by this request because the department had refused to make the house habitable for Jacob Sark some years previous; furthermore, there was no concern for its state of repair while the ferryman and his family lived there.

When John J. learned of the department's decision to dismiss him, he wrote what might be called his apologia, modelled on that of the great Greek philosopher Socrates, as reported by his pupil Plato. John began by reminding the department that he had served in the great war: "From December 1914 I served our King and Country in that great conflict both in France and Belgium." Then he expressed the hope that in the course of his services with the department he had never been found to be dishonest or untruthful in any way. He noted that he was aware that complaints had been filed against him and he was sorry to report that "the one who made those complaints is now in a mental hospital in Charlottetown." He hoped his accusers, who were men of unreliable character, would pardon him for writing about them in his own defense. John then described the so-called brawl in which he was assaulted. The incident, he said, was a source of great embarrassment to himself, his wife and his family. In the interest of justice and fair play, for which he had fought less than ten years before, he suggested that "an investigation be made by an impartial and disinterested party," and humbly begged the department to reconsider their decision.

The upshot was the re-instatement of John J. Sark as teacher. Again, so to speak, the captive had taken captive his captors, for on October 31, 1928, the new chief, after warning John of the need for exemplary conduct on the part of a teacher, agreed to give him another chance as teacher in the school!

In January 1929 an epidemic of influenza broke out on Lennox Island and the school had to be closed for a considerable period of time. There was little assistance from the federal health authorities who were responsible for the health of the Micmac Indians on the Reserve. A provincial sanatorium was being constructed in Charlottetown, but as yet there was no Department of Public

Health. Once again, Elsie Sark stepped forward to serve as nurse, where needed. Her spirit of forbearance was remarkable as she ministered to the needs of a community in which unemployment, poverty and tuberculosis were daily increasing. She was particularly disturbed when influenza claimed as one of its victims Annie May Sark. Although Elsie's work was well known of in Ottawa, there does not seem to have been any official recognition of her years of volunteer work in health services. Certainly she received no remuneration. The elders recall how hard-earned products from her own small family farm were distributed regularly to the sick, the poor and the needy. Her commitment to service and dedication to the mission that was carved out for her were never more evident than during that difficult year. It was a year for giving and Elsie Sark responded in her usual unselfish way.

On August 18, Elsie gave birth to a third daughter, who was baptised Kathleen Joan on September 1 of the same year. When, just two months and ten days later the Wall Street stock market crashed, Elsie knew in her heart a time for sacrifice was close at hand. There were no regrets on her part for staying on the Reserve, now that a decade had passed since their tentative decision.

10 | Witness to Survival

For the Sark family the thirties came in like a lamb but went out like a lion. Despite differences in temperament, outlook, and lifestyle, John Sark worked hard for his brother during the election campaign in the summer of 1930. When Jacob successfully defeated the incumbent Chief Isaac Peters by an overwhelming majority of the votes cast, there was great rejoicing.

Not only did the outcome of the election bring psychological relief to the Reserve as a whole, it marked the beginning of a new decade of hope for Elsie and her family. It was a time to relax! Elsie looked forward with gratitude to a few years of peace when she could give full attention to her ever-growing family, and possibly to rebuild a united community. For her part, she would continue to demonstrate her love and dedication as wife, mother and nurse within the intimate circle of her own family and, when required, throughout the community at large. Actually Elsie's straightforward unaffected witness to love of God and neighbour during this decade is very alive in the hearts, minds and memories of all who know her personally or heard of her accomplishments from afar.

"Her whole life was her family," was a statement reiterated by her contemporaries on the mainland. In fact, the demands on Mrs. Sark's expertise as nurse gradually dwindled during the thirties, when the provincial health authorities assumed more and more of the responsibility for health care on the Reserve. This co-operative effort on the part of provincial and federal governments left Elsie relatively free to concentrate her time and energies on her own home, her husband and her young family.

During this period when she thought her child-bearing years were behind her, she gave birth to three more healthy children. A blue-eyed blonde-haired daughter was born on the first day of September, 1931, and was baptized Mary Iris a few days later in the Mission Church of St. Anne. Before this "angelic golden-headed little girl" was three years old, Elsie conceived again. When she was eight months into her pregnancy John T. Sark, her father-in-law, was stricken with paralysis and died on January 7, 1934. His sickness and death was a great blow to the forty-two-year-old Elsie. Their love and respect for each other began the instant she set foot on the Reserve some sixteen years before and had developed over the years. She no doubt prayed to St. Joseph, to whom she had acquired a great devotion, that the emotional ordeal connected with the ex-chief's passing would not have an adverse effect on the infant she was carrying in her womb.

When, therefore, she gave birth to a healthy baby boy, she was ecstatic. There was no question regarding the name to be given this child born on February 7, 1934. John Joseph Thomas Sark was named for his paternal grandfather and Saint Joseph his protector!

Almost four years later, when Elsie was well past her forty-fifth birthday, another child was conceived. Dr. Stewart, her long-time doctor friend from Tyne Valley, was well aware of potential problems because of her age so he arranged admittance to the Charlottetown Hospital when the time came for her to deliver. The oldest daughter, Martha, who had been attending a boarding school conducted by the Sisters of the Congregation of Notre Dame in Miscouche, was summoned to keep house, temporarily. On November 3, 1937, while John Sark was on his lunch hour, a telegram arrived announcing the arrival of a baby boy. Martha recalls that when her father read the message, he danced a jig on the kitchen floor. His one regret, she said, was that his son was not born one day earlier: "Why wasn't he born on my birthday?" her father commented.

Weather conditions were uncertain at this particular time of the year, so Elsie—woman of faith—took no chances in delaying the christening of her new baby. She had good friends residing in Charlottetown, on nearby Pownal Street—Father John A.'s niece

91

and her husband Mary and Patrick (Packy) Murnaghan. Accordingly, arrangements were made to have Charles Hubert baptized in St. Dunstan's Basilica on November 14, 1937, with Reverend W.A. Keefe officiating and with the Murnaghans as the sponsors.

The birth of Charlie marked the end of Elsie Sark's child-bearing. From her perspective, however, child-rearing was a far more complex and demanding responsibility. She was at heart a homemaker who firmly believed that a woman's place was in the home. Staying at home and raising children was a career through which she could quietly assist in moulding the next generation. Christian family living was both a responsibility and a challenge which she did not take lightly.

Mrs. Sark's ideas on the upbringing of children were well known and highly lauded by her neighbours in the surrounding white communities. These ideas harked back to her own childhood where children were to be seen, not heard; where respect for parents and elders was a virtue of paramount importance; where children, far from being coddled, were expected to share in the household tasks and responsibilities at an early age. She realized that her ideas were in sharp contrast to the Micmac concept of child-rearing, in which children were welcomed as gifts from God, valued as persons and given the freedom to do pretty much as they pleased. Even moral weaknesses and transgressions evoked compassion, not condemnation and punishment, from parents and elders alike.

Fortunately, John Sark could relate to both traditions. He agreed with his wife that responsibility needed to be developed in children, but drawing on his many years of experience as a teacher of elementary school children, he was not at all sure how this could best be done. He himself had learned the value of discipline during his years in sport. Before the war he was accused of being too strict with the children in the school. After having been through the discipline of the army he felt, on the one hand, that the laissez-faire attitude adopted by his own people was an open invitation to deterioration of character and, more ultimately, to social disaster, and on the other hand, he knew from experience it was possible to invite rebellion by making discipline too strict and coercion too severe. In the classroom he tried to resolve the dilemma by dealing with his pupils on an individual basis, by prudently coping with each problem as it arose. The parents did not always appreciate his disciplinary measures and conflict ensued. In the home, when he tried to balance discipline and freedom, he had problems also.

It is possible to reconstruct from reminiscences of the Sark family, and their close friends, that child-rearing practices in the Sark household focused on the development of the Victorian values of hard work, thrift, sobriety and respect. This obviously was Elsie's domain. Like most children of elementary school age on rural Prince Edward Island, the Sark children were expected to share in the endless daily tasks of the home and farm. Joan summed up the situation succinctly:

> At home we all had chores to do. The youngest was given the task of feeding the hens, collecting the eggs, carrying in the kindling. Later we would be required to milk the cows or work the separator, feed the calves and pigs, weed the garden, carry in the wood. Mom was always nearby to instruct and help. If we were ill, she would do those chores willingly herself.[1]

Martha remembers a rigorous daily schedule which altered according to the season. Each member of the family co-operated.

> Daddy rose at 5 a.m., knelt upright on a chair in the kitchen to say his morning prayers, lit or stoked the stove, went to the barn to feed the livestock, clean the stables, etc., before breakfast. The oatmeal porridge was prepared the night before.... I can see Daddy coming home from school to plough or harrow the fields.... After supper the children would get the cows, milk them and separate the milk. One task I did not appreciate was washing the separator. There were all those little discs to be washed, dried and put back in place. Mom never missed checking each part for cleanliness. During the winter months the children were responsible for bringing in the kindling and wood for the stove, pumping water for the horses and cows— the horses were very fussy! Then we would take our lanterns to the barn, climb up to the loft and fork the hay down to the animals below. It was a lot of fun![2]

Rebecca recalls that her mother was always gainfully occupied, that work was second-nature to her. Even after the regular day's work was completed, she was busy hooking mats, sewing or mending clothes, knitting socks or mittens, crocheting coverings for furnishings. The work-ethic was so strong, she was always too busy to join in the children's games. "I regret," Becky said, "that Mom did not take more time to read to us as children." For Elsie, the doer, reading was probably a luxury!

Training in responsibility began in the cradle. If, for example, a child cried after being put to bed or on awaking from sleep, Elsie believed it was badness on the part of the child; the child was looking for attention. She was adamant that this behaviour should be ignored. The children recall that their mother consistently turned a deaf ear to their cries and continued with whatever task she was engaged in, oblivious to the wails from the floor above. At such times their father would quietly sneak up the back stairs and attempt to alleviate the cause of the disturbance in one way or another: by lifting the child out of the crib and holding him or her in his arms, by softly singing a lullaby, by giving a treat.

A public health nurse recalled one occasion when she was holding a clinic on Lennox Island, the youngest child Charlie—"He couldn't have been more than two years of age," she said—was up in a tree. Afraid he would fall and injure himself, she alerted Mrs. Sark to the situation. In a quiet, self-contained English voice Mrs. Sark said, "Not to worry!" Her philosophy was if he managed to climb up, he would find his way back down! Charlie himself as a teenager recalls being caught with cigars. His mother's response was: "Sonny, if you can afford them, you can smoke them."

Each of the girls in turn had the responsibility of looking after the younger sisters and brothers when their mother was away from home on business of one kind or another, such as purchasing groceries and supplies from the Port Hill corner store just across the one-mile strip of water or ice, or marketing farm products in the larger Tyne Valley centre up the river, or assisting a neighbour as midwife, or working in the post office. When Martha, the oldest girl, went to boarding school the task of keeping house fell to Rebecca. When Joan's turn came she had to contend with her younger brothers who were not particularly fond of farm work; on occasion they were successful in being able to bribe her to milk the cows for them!

This aspect of their training was an essential part of the upbringing of girls in the Indian culture. The idea was that as teenagers, girls were presumably ready to assume the roles of wives and mothers.

Example was an integral part of the training process. It was not necessary for Mrs. Sark to preach thrift; her example did not go unnoticed. The children were always well-fed, but they knew food was not to be wasted. They produced most of their own vegetables, milk, eggs and butter on the small family farm; other staple foods were procured by marketing surplus farm products. The girls recall that when they complained about having to eat the crust on the bread on the grounds it was hard, their mother was quick to retort, "It's harder where there's none to eat!" Again, the children were always well-clothed. Their mother made all their clothing and they knew they were expected to take care of it. There were clothes for Sunday, which were taken off after Mass and carefully hung in the cupboard in readiness for the following week. There were clothes for school, which were to be exchanged for work or play clothes immediately after school hours. Martha recalls how her mother bleached Robin Hood flour bags and used the material for various items of clothing. Sister Florence McTague, CSM, a great friend of Mrs. Sark in later years, observed:

> When it came to making purchases, she knew bargains. One fall she bought a large amount of plaid material, suitable for making winter dresses for her daughters. She made so many outfits that the material became unpopular, but, Mrs. Sark, being as persuasive as she was thrifty, succeeded in coaxing the girls to wear the dresses until they were worn out.[3]

Sarah Tuplin remembers how her Aunt Elsie went to Tyne Valley prior to Saint Anne's Day to purchase gingham for new dresses. "She sewed buttons on my dress and made beautiful button holes," Sarah remarked. It was no secret that Mrs. Sark was an accomplished seamstress and made most of her own clothes. Martha recalls she could make one hat into a number of different styles by adjusting a feather one year, a ribbon another year, tilting the brim on another occasion. The same was true for a dress or coat. She would put a fur collar on, take it off, adjust a button and produce a variety of designs in a seemingly effortless manner. The girls were well aware that their mother knew how to dress and were proud of the fact that she was always well-dressed and well-groomed. Martha was particularly proud of the fact that her mother designed her own patterns for quilts and floor mats, many of which are keepsakes in the homes of her married brothers.

Instruction and guidance on how to behave were important components in the upbringing of children in the Sark household. Children needed to be taught manners and morals and told what was right and wrong. If caught in wrong-doing, punishment was meted out on the spot. The children recall many an occasion. "If we misbehaved in church," for example, "we were taken to the vestibule and spanked there and then." As the girls became teenagers their activities were carefully monitored and chaperoned. Mrs. Bessie

McNeil recalls that occasionally Becky was allowed to stay over-night with her in Tyne Valley; it was well known that her aunt, Mrs. Sheldon Sharpe, was also very strict! According to Charlie, one never lied to Elsie. He tells the story of a hangover he had after an impromptu party to celebrate a championship in hockey. "Who bought it?" his mother asked. There was no sense in beating about the bush—she knew!

Discipline was no less strict in the school. According to Becky,

> If Daddy said "no" that meant NO. Lessons in school had to be exact; no half-measures were accepted. Others felt we did well because Daddy was the teacher. This was not so; it was mother who insisted we did our homework. Actually Daddy was more strict with his own children in the classroom and school. He felt we should be an example for the other pupils.
>
> He insisted we be punctual. If we went out to recess, we had to be back promptly when the bell rang. If we needed to be excused to leave the room to use the outdoor toilets or to get a drink at the outside pump, we had to ask to be excused. If we were not back promptly, he checked.[4]

According to Ray, his father was easy-going by nature but if a matter of principle were at stake, there was no compromising. Martha recalls that when the parents did not see eye-to-eye on a point of discipline, "Daddy would call her Maud—Maud the donkey!" Although their mother was seen as the domineering and aggressive partner who ruled the roost, John in his inimitable way could tease or charm his wife into accepting his or the children's points of view. As parents, the romantic John and the realistic Elsie made a great team. They were able to reconcile their differences and blend the virtues of stability and adaptability into the daily conduct of their home.

Training in the moral virtues was firmly rooted in religion and once again the parents were exemplars for their children. In those pre-Vatican II days, the basic guidelines were the Ten Commandments of God and the six precepts of the Church. The children vividly recall the many ways the faith was manifested in practice. Martha, for example, remembers that when Mass was celebrated only once a month in the mission chapel, "We travelled the nine or ten miles to the parish church in Grand River. Daddy and I would go one Sunday, Mom and Becky the next."

When Father Bennet Macdonald was assigned as curate to the aging Father John A. in 1933, Mass was celebrated every Sunday on Lennox Island. The time of the Mass would alternate with Grand River. One Sunday it would be scheduled for 8 a.m.; the following Sunday for 10 a.m. In later years, when there was a resident priest, Mass was celebrated on a daily basis and the Sark boys were always among the dependable altar boys.

Joan was particularly impressed by her mother's "marvellous faith and prayerfulness."

> Mother was very devoted to our religion. Each evening she would recite the rosary and evening prayers. At bedtime she would hear our prayers before she tucked us into bed.

Both Martha and Rebecca recall the priority given to devotions to the Blessed Virgin Mary during the month of May.

> We had to cease playing ball, or whatever activity we were engaged in, and go to the church at 6 p.m.—bare feet and all—to sing hymns to Our Lady and recite the rosary together. Daddy would kneel upright on the organ stool without support and hold up his fingers to indicate which number of Hail Mary was being recited.

Involvement in events connected with their religion left an indelible mark on the memories of the children. Becky recalled

> At Christmas, Mother and Daddy prepared the crib. They used a large wooden carton for the table on which the stable and figures were placed. Then they cut out large letters for the GLORIA IN EXCELSIS DEO to be hung over the scene. These letters were covered with sparkle and tinsel. The effect for Midnight Mass was beautiful.

Years later, Sister Mary Magdalen Connolly, CSM, referred to a similar scene. When electric lights were installed, they would be left burning on Christmas Eve until after Midnight Mass.

> It gave a postcard effect to watch the natives, lanterns in hand, make their way through the large flakes of snow to Midnight Mass. Eleven children made their first communion my first year there. The women sang the carols; the men sang the Latin Mass of the Angels.

There were many witnesses to the Sarks' involvement in church activities. John Sark served the church as organist and as choir director. His inspired singing is well-remembered.

Mrs. Sark's talents were along different lines. Becky recalls that her mother made hosts and prepared the vestments for liturgical celebrations. She also washed, starched and ironed the altar cloths and other linens and carefully pleated the albs and surplices.

She also taught the younger women how to perform these services, including her niece Sarah Tuplin, who felt privileged to assist in this preparation of the altar linens. Residents reminisce that she would heat flat irons on the stove, spread two blankets on the floor, cover them with a clean sheet, get down on her knees and iron the linens with great respect. According to Mrs. Tuplin,

> Before Elsie Sark came to Lennox Island, my grandmother Molly (Francis) Mitchell took care of the church and the priests. When she died Uncle Mick Francis' wife Maria—a woman of Acadian French origin—took over the care of the parochial house and the church. Aunt Elsie was younger and handier to the church. She must have offered to do it. She wanted to be a good Catholic, not a backward one. The Micmac attitude generally was "women are women and cannot be men....Stay back and let the men go forward. It's a man's place around the church." So when Aunt Elsie went inside the sanctuary, this was frowned upon by the Micmac men. They didn't like it; she was too pushy![5]

Mrs. Bessie MacNeil and other Anglo-Catholic friends viewed her "as a great church woman; her heart was in the church."

Father Bennet Macdonald, who was assigned to the Grand River parish as curate in 1933 and served as pastor (1936-1941) after Father John A.'s death, had great praise for Mrs. Sark. "She was a wonderful woman, a marvellous Catholic," he said.

> When I came to Lennox Island first, Mrs. Sark looked after the priests while they ministered to the people on Lennox Island. She prepared their meals, kept the house comfortable and saw that everything was spotlessly clean in the church and in readiness for services.
>
> It was tough in those days. We couldn't even have a drink of water before Mass. When the first Mass was scheduled for Lennox Island, I would go over the night before. She was a great help; she would have the house comfortable and everything in readiness for Mass. Often, especially around Easter, it was not safe to cross. One Easter Sunday I asked the Indians to come with horse and sleigh to get me;

I felt a car wouldn't be safe. They insisted the ice was solid enough, so I drove across with Johnny Francis. I had no fear when the Indians were with me.[6]

St. Anne's Day was another event during which the Sark parents were totally involved. Becky saw it this way:

> Daddy even slept all night in the community hall to ensure there were no thefts; Mom would feed us after Mass and leave us. For the rest of the day she was involved in a number of activities which altered from year to year. They ranged from serving in the ice-cream booth all day to feeding the priests and dignitaries and entertaining off-Reserve guests. At the end of the day's activities, we would have our special treats.

Important as these ministrations were, Mrs. Sark's primary concerns were of a spiritual nature. She and her husband, for example, were sponsors at the baptisms of countless children on and off the Reserve, all of whom bear testimony to the fact that she never forgot their birthdays! Sister Catherine Macdonald, CND, remembers when her sister Josephine's child was born in Port Hill on January 20, 1935, the seven-mile stretch of road to Grand River was completely blocked by snow. It was impossible to bring the newborn baby girl to St. Patrick's Church for christening. Mrs. Sark visited the MacDougall family and offered to come and get the baby and take her to Lennox Island to be baptized. Frank and his wife agreed, provided John and Elsie would consent to be the sponsors. And so it was that Pauline Marie MacDougall was welcomed into the Catholic Church by Father John A. at St. Anne's Mission Church on Lennox Island on February 10, 1935. Pauline (Mrs. Frank Harper of Halifax) will never forget the beautiful plaid dresses which she received from her generous godmother, some years later.

Sarah Tuplin recalls the incidents connected with making her First Communion when she was only eight years old:

> My mother was sick. I couldn't speak English very well as Micmac was spoken in my home. I wanted to go to confession, so I asked Aunt Elsie for help. She got her coat and hat took me to Church. Father John was there from Grand River.

The Sark girls—Martha and Rebecca—received the Sacrament of Confirmation on St. Anne's Day, July 26, 1931. They recall the festive occasion during which decked in white dresses and veils they accompanied Bishop O'Leary to the wharf after the ceremony. The following year, when the Eucharistic Congress was held in Miscouche, they were among the two or three boat loads of residents who attended the congress. Small wonder, then, that those two girls devoted their lives to the Church by joining religious orders. Religion was the top priority in the Sark household during their most formative years.

Elsie Sark was especially solicitous about her children's schooling. She was bound they were going to have the best education available in the region. It was a great disappointment, therefore, when Martha wanted to drop out of school in Grade VI. Being the oldest in the family, Martha had "missed a lot of school" looking after her younger brothers and sisters while her mother was attending to family or community business. Physically she was bigger than the other school children and at fourteen she was conscious of being older. The problem was solved when school inspector Hilda Gillis suggested to Mrs. Sark that Martha be sent to a private boarding school. And so it was that Martha Sark was registered in 1933 as a boarder at St. Joseph's Convent School in the village of Miscouche, about twenty-five miles from Lennox Island. Rebecca followed her there in 1937, Raymond in 1939, Joan in the 1940s.

Mrs. Sark settled for nothing less than the best. She arranged for the girls to take private music lessons while they were enroled in the convent school. The government provided some financial assistance, but the family was largely responsible for tuition and board. Piano lessons, of course, were one of the extras. For Elsie, this was money well invested. By 1938, Martha had passed the Matriculation Examinations and moved on to Prince of Wales College and Normal School; Becky followed her in 1940.

The mid-thirties were landmarked by a number of events which in turn were occasions for sorrow and joy in the Sark family and the residents of the Reserve generally. The deaths of ex-chief John Thomas Sark and Indian Agent John A. McDonald, in 1934 and 1936 respectively, marked the end of an era. John Thomas Sark had been the greatest public-relations figure the Micmacs of Prince Edward Island had ever known; Father John A. McDonald had been their devoted servant and spokesman for two decades. These losses were deeply felt by Elsie and John Sark for whom they had been trusted confidantes and counsellors over the years. For the young Chief Jacob Sark, he had lost his two great mentors, sources of prudence and wisdom.

Sandwiched between these two sorrowful occasions were two events, one joyful, the other glorious. The first brought with it an emotional high for Mrs. Sark. Buckingham Palace had forwarded to the Department of Indian Affairs in Ottawa a medal accompanied by the following instructions:

By Command
of
HIS MAJESTY THE KING
the accompanying Medal is forwarded
to
JOHN J. SARK
to be worn in commemoration of
Their Majesties' Silver Jubilee
6th May, 1935

This award was forwarded to Reverend J.A. McDonald, Indian Superintendent, by A.F. MacKenzie, Secretary for the Department of Indian Affairs, with the following letter dated May 1, 1935:

I am enclosing, herewith, a King's Silver Jubilee Medal.

This Medal has been conveyed to the Department through the Honourable the Secretary of State by command of His Majesty the King for presentation to John J. Sark to be worn in commemoration of Their Majesties' Silver Jubilee, May 6, 1935.

This honour is being conferred upon Mr. Sark in recognition of his services on behalf of his people and the State. Please make suitable arrangements for the presentation at as early a date as possible, convenient to yourself and the recipient.[7]

This recognition from King George V was a red-letter day for Elsie. She was proud of her English heritage. She recalled that her late father-in-law had been similarly recognized by Queen Victoria on the Diamond Jubilee. She knew John would accept the award humbly; for him, it was a sign of approval; for her, it was a well-deserved mark of prestige. Now that his drinking problem was well under control, she hoped this honour would re-affirm confidence in himself as a teacher and a leader in the community.

In the summer of that same year, Father John A., "a giant among men," celebrated his Golden Jubilee—the fiftieth anniversary of his ordination to the holy priesthood. The diocesan-wide celebration was centred in the parish headquarters, Grand River in July 29; however, the Sarks made sure that their well-beloved friend received a special tribute from the Micmacs of the St. Anne Mission, with a heartfelt message read by Chief Jacob Sark.

Elsie's turn for recognition came on December 27, 1936, in an article in the Summerside *Journal*, praising John Sark as "chieftain of Indian youth"; John, however, the article stated, gave the credit for his success to his English wife, a war bride.

Returning to Summerside after an official visit to the little island colony off the north coast of Prince Edward Island, Miss Hilda W. Gillis, Inspector of Schools, reported: "The teacher is an outstanding athlete and musician. The pupils showed aptitude in the mechanics of reading, writing and other school subjects. Singing is especially well taught in both Micmac and English."

"The teacher takes advantage of the Carnegie Library facilities and is well versed in the principles of teaching. The Indian pupils are apparently slow to grasp ideas when presented in English, but it is remarkable how well they remember what they receive and how thoroughly their work is done."

"Mr. Sark," the school inspector said, "has indeed a great experimental field in education. His work is satisfactory and commendable."

Then citing the "keen-eyed Indian teacher," the article continues,

In the eyes of his people his wife was a stranger and for a time unwelcome. "But the beauty of her nature, the unselfishness of her life and the affection she showered upon me won their everlasting affection."

The English woman has adapted herself to local customs and has become a leading spirit in the community.[8]

The praise was well earned for Elsie Sark's energies extended beyond the home and the parish to the health and welfare of the community at large. Mrs. Harold Brown, a lifelong friend, never ceased singing this woman's praises since 1937 when she proved to be her friend *par excellence.*

When my last baby was born, she was with me. The baby was not deformed, but his intestines were on the outside and nobody knew what to do. The minister's wife Mrs. Clark Davies said the operation had been performed successfully in England, but our baby only lived four days. He was a big baby and must have weighed twelve pounds. Mrs. Sark went to Summerside with my husband Harold, took the baby to the hospital and stayed all night by his side. The baby died at 4 a.m. the following morning, the first of April, Elsie's own birthday ... She came back to my home and stayed with me. She was my greatest comfort. I always loved her for what she did on that occasion, more than my own people. My sister-in-law from New York had sent me lovely things for the baby—more than for any other child. Mrs. Sark was expecting Charlie, so I gave everything to her.

The public health nurses who served Lennox Island during this decade attest to Mrs. Sark's generous support of community projects and her gracious hospitality.

Nurse Mary Darling (Mrs. Lou Roper), stationed in Alberton from 1938 to 1942, made three trips to Lennox Island during one year

I went once with Dr. Stewart from Tyne Valley. We went to the Sark home and were treated royally. We were invited to dinner. It happened to be Friday and she had cooked fish for the family. She cooked chicken specially for the visitors!

Mrs. Sark did a lot of work as nurse on the Reserve and surrounding region. She did charity, volunteer work, for which she was not paid a cent. She had no office and did not receive any official recognition for her labours.

We went to the school to test the children's eyes. I was taken by Mr. Sark. I can see how she fell for him! He was very handsome, had a melodious singing voice and played the piano. He must have looked stunning in uniform. He was a real gentleman. It was clear that he wanted all the children on the Reserve to have a good education. The school children sang the national anthem for us in Micmac.[9]

Proud of his heritage and eager to have his pupils display their expertise in their native tongue, music was a vehicle through which John could do this without inviting criticism from the authorities.

Ever since Elsie Sark assumed responsibility for nursing her husband back to health, she had been meticulous about cleanliness and good health habits in their home. It is probable that she was instrumental in setting up the Junior Red Cross Society which was operating in the day school as far back as 1931. No doubt, she encouraged her husband to push for a larger school to alleviate overcrowding and provide more air space and better accommodations for the pupils. Unfortunately, he always had to settle for *ad hoc* improvements: a new stove in 1930; additional desks in 1931; new readers and suitable cupboard in 1932; permission to build a shed, paint and repair the school and fix up the grounds in 1936; supplies, including towelling, window shades, soap, polish, brush and a pump, stove and toilets in 1937.

In sponsoring a drive to check tuberculosis in 1938, John Sark almost met his Waterloo! Again, this was to be the scenario of the thirties when he would be the villain of the piece. The results of the T.B. test showed 50 percent of the children were positive. This was the occasion for John Sark's old enemies, headed by Isaac Peters and others (who had no children attending school), to mount another smear campaign in an attempt to remove him from his position as school teacher. The strategy was to blame the school and the teacher for the state of the children's health and use this as the rationale for keeping the children home from school. Accordingly, in July 1938, a letter of complaint about the teacher was sent to the Indian Branch of the Department of Mines and Resources signed by thirty-six residents, including the teacher's own brother, Chief Jacob Sark, and his own sister, Mary Elizabeth (Mitchell) Thomas. The petition requested that a new teacher be appointed or steps be taken to have all the children sent to the residential school in Shubenacadie, Nova Scotia.

For Elsie Sark, this was a time for action! Unknown to her husband she wrote to the Department to throw "a little light on what the petition is all about." Her letter reads in part,

> We have four of our own children going to school, besides three others, and I know how those that are going to school are treated, in fact they always get the worst as an example to the other pupils. The parents say that they should not be kept in from recreation for punishment as it caused the children to develop TB; but I think if they were to clean their homes, and the janitor that is paid to keep the school clean would do his work, the school would be healthier than their homes.[10]

It was her contention that the main reason for the petition was "spite from some of the uneducated people that are always finding fault and trying to make mischief" especially when they are under the influence of drink, and "there is lots of it going on here right now." According to Father Bennet, John no longer had a drinking problem. Another reason she cited was the children at Shubena-cadie are kept in food and clothes. This solution would enable the parents to draw "the full supplies at home so they can loaf around and have no bother..."

Elsie was not the only one who rallied to her husband's defense. Father Bennet Macdonald wrote to the department on August 23:

> I wish to testify that the teacher here, Mr. J.J. Sark, is most capable, that he is an influence for good among the Indian children and that he is a credit to the Indians of Prince Edward Island. I believe that those who signed the petition for his removal were not acting in the best interests of the tribe, so I trust your Department will carry out its usual thorough investigation before action is taken.

The Department of Education on Prince Edward Island was asked to make a special inspection of the Lennox Island School, particularly the work of the teacher during the past year. Merritt E. Callaghan, BA, was assigned the task. After making the inspection on October 24, he reported that the only children in attendance were the teacher's.

> The school was very clean and tidy and Mr. Sark seems to be very interested in his work. I think that some pressure should be brought to bear on the parents of the children who are not attending school.

This report corroborated inspectors' reports which had been uniformly good over John J. Sark's twenty-four years as teacher in the school.

Back in July, Indian Agent Mr. N.A. McDougall had been asked personally to conduct an investigation of the alleged grievances and report his findings to the department. On August 9, the agent wrote that any time he visited the Lennox Island School he found everything in order and the school well kept, adding that he certainly did not wish to see it closed.

The grievances were not of a serious nature, he noted. When he checked with Mr. Sark regarding his keeping pupils in during recreation hours, the teacher's response was that, in many cases, it has made them get their work done, which otherwise would not have been done. The agent noted in his letter to Mr. Philip Phelan that the Sark family were bright and projected that Martha would succeed her father as teacher at the Lennox Island school.

In a later report dated October 8, the agent concluded, after describing his contacts with the residents of the Reserve, that the grievances could be boiled down to one word, spite. It was John Sark himself who alerted the agent to the fact his own brother Jacob, the Chief, was influenced by people who did not have children in the school.

Actually John Sark had great sympathy for his brother, coping with the problems of unemployment, alcoholism and poverty which accompanied the Depression years, as well as the health situation. Jacob had lost his second wife to tuberculosis in 1927 and his only daughter less than one month later. At that time, he and his father were aware of Jacob's leadership qualities and urged him to let his name stand for the position of chief. Now he was well into his third term as chief, was happily married to Alma Cormier—a woman of French descent from Petit Roch, New Brunswick—and he was well settled on the Reserve with his young family.

John confided the real reason to Mr. R.A. Hoey, Superintendent of Welfare and Training, Ottawa, in a long letter dated October 5.

> This petition was drawn up and sent through spite and jealousy. This is why Indians in our Reserve do not get ahead. As soon as one is improving his house or his farm they all turn on him. There are some who do not do any work. They are where they were years ago and they cannot bear to see others getting ahead.
>
> Last year we had six families sending their children to school. I visited them, met them and chatted with them. I was well received. They told me time and time again they found no fault with me or our school. It is our Chief Jacob Sark backed by these few agitators.

In the course of the letter he documented the fact that he was in a losing situation inasmuch as the Chief was *ex officio* truant officer and his wife, Alma was janitress. He had conscientiously reported periodically to the Chief during which he underscored what he considered to be a number of serious complaints regarding the poor attendance of children, the lack of cleanliness of the school, the misuse of the school building when it was made available for evening meetings, the theft of school property, misbehaviour of children, and so on.

> All these I reported to our Chief Jacob as he is a Chief, truant officer and sees our Agent every week. That is the only thing I remember ever being guilty of. Instead of Chief Jacob Sark correcting his children, he kept them home from school, instead of correcting his wife, he took her part and turned against our family.

With regard to the present apparent impasse, he wrote:

> The children are anxious to go to school, but I understand the parents to say they were expecting a letter from Ottawa. I was talking to Chief Jacob Sark, asked him if the Department were to allow me

106

to continue to teach would his children go. He answered yes and willingly. He only wished now that everything was all settled.

The reason I asked him was this: when I asked the other families if their children were coming to school, their answers were: We do not find any fault with you or your school. When the Chief Jacob's children go, they will all go.

Finally, among other things, John Sark briefly reviewed his record of service:

I served under three Agents, three Inspectors and they all gave me a good report and found my work of very high order. In rain or shine, winter or summer, I have my school operating with the best I have in me. One year, in Father John's time, all the schools were closed on P.E.I. but our humble school. I am a Catholic not only by name and it is through my sacred religion I want to serve my God honestly, to our Indian Department, to my fellow man and to myself.

Before the end of January 1939, not only were the children on the Reserve attending school, many of those enroled in the residential school in Shubenacadie were returning to the Day School on Lennox Island. Another milestone had been reached, albeit not without suffering.

11 | The Price of Love

As the years passed and her children grew further from home, Elsie Sark realized that her own disciplined upbringing had prepared her for a life marked by vicissitudes. She appreciated, too, that her husband's constant love and fidelity supported her through days, weeks, months, even years of loneliness and rejection on the part of the people who continued to see her as an outsider. She was grateful to God that John had been able to surmount his personal and professional problems. His easy-going nature and keen sense of humour, coupled with the consistent encouragement of his family and friends, had carried him through many a crisis. But what about their children? Were they morally and spiritually fortified to cope with the realities of ostracism and racism? These were real concerns that needed to be addressed now that they were beginning to leave the Reserve to further their education.

There was no problem in the immediate environment. The Sarks and the inhabitants of Lennox Island generally got along well with their white neighbours in the small communities on the mainland. But Elsie was aware of the patronizing and depreciatory attitudes toward the natives that surreptitiously permeated society at large, attitudes which were written into the official Indian policies at the federal level. From her perspective as a Christian, it was intolerable, and she used each opportunity as it arose to make her own position clear. Sister Florence McTague, CSM, recounts Mrs. Sark's response on one occasion when she detected racist behaviour:

> None of the natives owned cars, and, for their infrequent shopping trips to Summerside, a group of them would hire a taxi from the Port Hill wharf to town. On one occasion, as she sat in the car with two of her Indian friends, she saw a lady start to the car, hurriedly back out and say, "Oh, Indians." Just as hurriedly Mrs. Sark followed her, and, catching up with her said, "They are just as good as you are."[1]

To offset attitudes of racial intolerance, such as these, Elsie urged her husband to try to stretch the horizons of the school children by encouraging them to stay in school so that they would be prepared to take their places with dignity in the white world beyond the Reserve. For John, the struggle was uphill all the way. Elsie supported him even when the battle seemed to be a losing one, and he did not give up.

As teacher, John Sark knew that he was in a unique position to help the Indian children develop a positive self-concept which would enable them to compete academically with their fellow Islanders. In athletics—baseball, football, hockey—they excelled as a team and as individuals, many a Micmac boy won medals in competitive sports. Elsie kept reminding them that to be successful in Canadian society, schooling was a *sine qua non*. Interested as she was in his coaching the young boys, as school teacher his primary responsibility was to prepare them for the professions and the work world as a whole. The textbooks provided for use in the school were at variance with Micmac values; however, he himself was able to relate to the Anglo-Saxon values conveyed in these books and was able to translate and interpret them in such a way as not to alienate the children from their mother tongue and native culture. He was especially sensitive to the fact that his own children's heritage was double-rooted in the Anglo-Saxon and Algonquin races and he did all in his power to transcend potential cross-cultural conflict. It was a tall order and a potentially explosive one; however, he was satisfied that in the long run it seemed to be paying off in the case of his own family.

Schooling, however, was not a priority for the Micmac Indians during the dark days of the Depression when poverty, disease and unemployment were ever-present. Survival was the first priority, and boys gladly dropped out of school to go fishing with their father, while the girls stayed home to assist their mothers and the neighbours with routine household tasks. In any case, they felt intuitively that regimentation in the classroom was no substitute for the freedom to roam at will; book knowledge was a far cry from the knowledge acquired from the contemplation of the wonders of nature. During those years, as a group, the Micmac seemed to have settled for their perceived status as second-class citizens. They camped along the railroad tracks or trekked around the province peddling their baskets and other Indian wares from door to door, gratefully accepting any food which was given them in charity. From their perspective, Elsie Sark was "just a squaw like any other" and they were "just Indians" forced to eke out a precarious existence from one day to the next.[2]

It was one thing for Elsie to try to teach her children to cope with rejection from the non-native population beyond the Reserve, quite another thing to help them deal with the experience of being spurned by their relatives, friends, peers. During the summer of 1938 she tried to side-step the problem by ensuring that her children were involved at all times in worthwhile activities in the home and community. Thanks to her good management and despite the Depression, the value of their property steadily increased. Besides their home, they had a horse, a cow, a mower, a truck wagon and horse rake which enabled them to be relatively self-sufficient. By 1942 the Soldier Settlement was paid in full and the Sarks had a clear title to their property. As a family they co-operated to achieve this goal; during the vacation periods in the summer the whole family participated in the daily jobs within the home.

This particular summer, 1938, there were additional chores to be accomplished within the family circle besides the annual tasks associated with the elaborate preparations for the St. Anne's Day celebration. Ray and Joan were preparing to receive the Sacrament of Confirmation on August 14; this meant extra classes and homework in religion. Martha would be off to Charlottetown in September to attend Prince of Wales College and Normal School. She would be boarding at Notre Dame Convent on Sydney Street along with most out-of-city Catholic girls aspiring to become teachers; the Sisters had already given her a list of preliminary "musts" which had to be attended to. Rebecca would be returning to the convent school in Miscouche after Labour Day; she was expected to spend her free time perfecting her musical skills on the piano. When, however, the excitement of the summer activities was over and the two oldest girls had left the Reserve, the next three in line—eleven-year-old Ray, nine-year-old Joan and seven-year-old Iris—had to face the fact that they were the only children attending the local school. It was a bizarre example of racism which they would have to learn to live with from time to time.

The year 1939 proved to be historically eventful. On May 15 their Majesties King George VI and Queen Elizabeth arrived in Charlottetown, their first stop on a month-long tour of Canada. The royal visit had special significance for the Sark family, so when the royal couple visited Summerside, they were on hand to witness the event. Less than four months later, Canada joined forces with Britain in the Second World War.

The day the formal announcement was made regarding the declaration of war, the schoolteachers from East Prince County were assembled in Summerside for the annual convention sponsored by the Teachers' Federation. Sister Mary Henry Mulligan, CSM, who was present, recalls the events of the day clearly:

> There was a teachers' convention held in the old Summerside High School the day the second world war was declared. About mid-afternoon when sessions were in full swing, the announcement was made. Everything pertaining to the convention came to a standstill; everyone was shocked. After a few moments a message was sent over the loudspeaker. Everyone was to assemble in the school auditorium. John J. Sark from Lennox Island, the only person in the entire group who had served in World War I, was on the stage ready to speak. His very presence attracted the attention of everyone present.
>
> John Sark was a beautiful person. In all my long life of listening and being bored with talks, I have never heard anything more interesting than the impromptu talk he gave us that day. He was a powerful speaker and had a charismatic effect on his hearers as he fired zeal in us as a group to get out and do everything within our power to make the war effort a success.[3]

A resolution was passed recording their loyalty and patriotism to their king and country. John J. Sark's own sentiments about war had been expressed some years before. "I hate war," he said, "and the consequences of it, but I have to thank God for the world upheaval that brought me the English girl and the children that now surround us."[4]

One can only speculate on Elsie's thoughts as she watched twenty-seven young Indians from Lennox Island enlist for service. Had her son John Reuben lived, he would probably have been among the first volunteers. Her sister Nellie's planned trip to Canada would now be postponed. Whatever her feelings, Elsie the realist lost no time on idle thoughts. Her daughters recall how she regularly prepared parcels containing sugar and other rationed items for her sister in England.

The war years were undoubtedly the most memorable period of Elsie Sark's entire life, for she was called upon to prove the depth of her love for God and her family not on foreign soil, but on her home territory. No sooner had Martha graduated from Prince of Wales College and Normal School with her teaching license in 1940 when she made known her intention to give her life to God by joining the congregation of the Sisters of Notre Dame that fall. It would mean leaving Lennox Island and travelling to Montreal where the Motherhouse of the congregation was located. Elsie was elated, on the one hand, that her oldest daughter answered the call to the religious life; on the other hand, she was lonesome and downhearted after Martha left.

Sister Vera McLellan, CND, recalled that Elsie was extremely lonely and often sought the company of the Sisters at the Miscouche Convent.

While Elsie was struggling with these mixed emotions of pride and loneliness she was faced with a tragic experience—the loss of her little errand girl, eleven-year-old Iris. Many people in the area were saddened that the "dear little golden-haired, blue-eyed girl"— "a sweet little child"—had died of a ruptured appendix on October 17, 1941. "What a terrible thing to lose a little girl" was the comment reiterated by all who recalled the incident forty-five years after it happened. Public Health Nurse Mary Roper said that at the time the ice wasn't safe and it was impossible to cross by boat to get her to the doctor in Tyne Valley or the hospital in Summerside.

Friends, with tears in their eyes, remembered all the details. According to a great family friend Mrs. Jessie Brown:

> When Iris died, I went to the wake and funeral with my sister-in-law. I was never in such a lovely wake house. Those people came in and sang hymns all night long. Mr. Sark accompanied them on the piano. It was really beautiful. I remember especially that they sang the "Te Deum." It was a very cold night but the Indians sang in relays all night and through the morning.

Bernetta and I stayed overnight. Father John A. McDonald was our parish priest, so we slept over in the priest's house. Elsie, despite her own bereavement, took charge of everything. She was a marvellous woman.[5]

There was no prolonged mourning, for the "Te Deum" had said it all.

The following spring Rebecca graduated from Prince of Wales College and Normal School and was successful in obtaining a teaching position in a white community on the mainland. The first half-year she taught in Ellis River; the second half in Poplar Grove, near Lot 11. After that experience, Rebecca knew that teaching was not for her! When, therefore, she struggled with a religious vocation it was clear to her that the call was not to a teaching order. And so, in the fall of 1943, she joined the diocesan congregation of the Sisters of St. Martha whose Motherhouse was in Charlottetown.

By the time Rebecca left home, Martha had already made her religious profession and returned to Prince Edward Island as Sister Catherine of Sienna. Here she taught for the next two decades, her first assignment being the convent school in Tignish. Rebecca, Sister Ann Celestine in religion, pronounced her religious vows in 1945. Like her own mother she chose to serve the people of God through nursing, and she proceeded to Windsor, Ontario, where she earned a diploma in nursing.

Within the brief span of three years, Elsie had, so to speak, lost three daughters. Joan was the only girl at home; she, too, was enroled as a boarder in the Miscouche Convent School in 1943. Ray had just completed three years there and was registered for high school at St. Dunstan's College, his father's alma mater. By the fall of 1943, the two youngest boys were the only Sark children living on the Reserve during the school year. Education was a big investment for the Sarks.

While Elsie was carefully monitoring the education and careers of her children she continued to be the gracious hostess to all visitors to the island. During the summer of 1940, while Martha and Rebecca were still at home, one of their professors from Prince of Wales College stopped overnight on Lennox Island while he was making a trip around Prince Edward Island by canoe. Professor Redden wrote of this experience in his work, *My Canoe and I*.

And so, next day, inside Fish Island across Malpeque Bay, past Bird Island, and ashore at the southern tip of Lennox Island just at sunset... An elderly man... invited me to come with him to his house and have supper. He identified himself as John LaBobe...

I told John that I was anxious to get before dark to the home of John Sark, whose wife I had learned was an English girl... After what seemed a long time, John and I suddenly emerged into a small open field. Before us shone the light of a house and coming through the window we heard the sound of a piano.

The pianist, one of the Sark girls (was it Martha or was it Rebecca?) [sic], was too shy to play for me, so her father sat down and played, though he had no musical training. He had never heard of Liebestraum; I whistled a few bars and he played them right after me.

From Mrs. Sark I learned that he had become a teacher by attending St. Dunstan's and had been a crack football player there. A finer-looking man I have never seen, nor a more hospitable man have I met. Fine parents and lovely children, and to one little boy, Jackie, I was particularly attracted.

Mrs. Sark gave me a bed that night in the house of a non-resident priest and next morning fed me a hearty breakfast; the taste of the crisp bacon I still recall.[6]

Another instance of her gracious hospitality was cited by Sister Mary Henry, CSM, who knew Mrs. Sark well. She and Sister Carmelita Soloman were teaching catechism in Grand River parish during the early forties. On St. Anne's Day, Father Bennet brought them over to Lennox Island for Sunday Mass. It was long before the causeway was in place. According to Sister,

We were crossing in the ferry boat from Port Hill wharf when it began to rain as hard as it could rain. We had no umbrellas, no protection whatsoever. You can imagine what we looked like! Forebands, guimpes and all the paraphernalia the Sisters used to wear were soaking wet. We wondered what to do. We could not go to church with our clothes in that condition. Mrs. Sark came to the rescue. She very quietly ushered us into her home, seated us in one of the bedrooms, dried our clothes, starched and ironed our linens. In no time we went to Mass looking the same as we were when we left Grand River two hours before.[7]

Interviews with Mrs. Sark's contemporaries are replete with stories in which she emerges as the fairy godmother. Anyone whose life was touched by her in any way during those years claims to have been enriched by the experience. For the Sark children, there was nothing extraordinary about those ministrations. They flowed spontaneously from a way of life which had its source in a deep and abiding religious faith which she possessed long before she met their father and which sustained her through the many trials and tribulations of life on the Reserve. It had brought her through the emotional crises associated with the deaths of John Reuben and Iris, the departures of Martha and Rebecca, the discord and dissension occasioned by in-laws. Faith was a gift which she valued in her own life and to which she gave witness through her service to others regardless of creed, class, or race.

As Elsie Sark approached her fiftieth birthday, life on the Reserve was relatively quiet and peaceful. Mr. W.M. Arnell, the Inspector of Indian Affairs, had visited Lennox Island in July, 1941, and was well satisfied with the status quo. That fall, Father A. Oswald Murphy replaced Father Bennet McDonald as pastor of St. Patrick parish in Grand River, with responsibility for the St. Anne Mission on Lennox Island. A year later there was another change in personnel. Mr. J.E. Daly took over the position of Indian Agent. As postmistress Mrs. Sark had occasion to meet these newcomers and in her English way, born of good manners, made them feel perfectly at home. She was pleased to learn that after visiting the school on November 3, 1942, the agent "found everything running smoothly under the capable guidance of the teacher J.J. Sark."

It was also encouraging to see that efforts were being made that year to provide a permanent supply of willow canes for basket making by setting apart a sector of the island for the production of Welsh willows. When Father John A. McDonald was agent, large supplies of willow were brought over from New Brunswick "by the carload"; this present endeavour was an attempt to make the Indians self-sufficient in this regard.

There was more good news when on July 14, 1943, Justice Arsenault and Mr. McPhee, trustees of the Lady Wood estate accompanied the agent to Lennox Island and expended $1,200 for painting the church inside and outside and repairing the floor and foundation of the community hall. Things were beginning to look up economically and socially! By the end of 1944, Father Murphy had completed the parish census and had reported the following statistical data for that year. There were 25 families living on Lennox Island, 110 souls, 21 school children, 4 baptisms, 6 first communions, 21 confirmations and 4 deaths. That year, however, had been another tension-filled one for Elsie!

For five years there had been peace in the family. On January 18, 1944, when Agent J.E. Daly visited the school the attendance was good and everything was running smoothly. Two months later, following another school visit, he reported that the teacher was doing good work but that Chief Jacob Sark was not sending his children to school because of a grievance with his brother. "They can't get along," he wrote. "Some change will have to be made." Elsie could not bear to entertain the prospect of her husband's "losing face," so to speak, at this stage of his teaching career. She tried to assess the situation objectively, and as she pondered the situation, it gradually dawned on her that this particular skirmish, like the preceding ones in the twenties and thirties, was simply the continuation of a family feud which extended back historically for at least one hundred years.

The Sark family was the first warm, close-knit family she had known. She admired them for their loyalty to each other as a family and had convinced herself that it was she, "an outsider," who was the latent source of the tensions between her husband and his brother. Now it was clear that the Sarks—born leaders that they were—thrived on tension.

When school re-opened after the summer holidays in September 1944, John J. Sark was still at the helm. He was about to begin his twenty-fifth year of continuous teaching in the Lennox Island Indian Day School, and it was to be his last! In the quarter report ending March 1945 the agent proudly referred to the five recent graduates who were making good progress in other educational institutions on Prince Edward Island. Regarding the local situation he wrote, "At present all the children on the Reserve are attending school and the teacher is making a great effort to improve conditions." The effort proved to be too much. On Tuesday, April 17, 1945, after having taught school all day, John Sark quietly passed away. He had returned home from school as usual, had supper with Elsie and the two boys followed by evening prayers. About 9 p.m. while relaxing in his armchair, he was stricken with a heart attack that proved to be fatal. John James Sark at the age of 56 years, 5 months, 15 days was dead. His niece Sarah (Mitchell) Tuplin vividly recalls her observations of her uncle as she watched him going to school the very day of his death.

> Uncle John was draggy the day he died. It was a very cold day. He had his overcoat on and was walking to school. Usually he had a brisk military walk but he was walking very slowly that day. At

the time I was expecting a baby and I watched him from my window. I told my mother, "I bet he'll keep teaching until he drops dead." That night it was rough and dark; the wind was blowing hard and strong. At 9 p.m. the church bells tolled. (There were no telephones on Lennox Island in those days.) The bells were announcing the death of John Sark. Everyone on the Reserve was shocked; so were his friends, the parish priest and the Indian Agent...[8]

"The loss of this man," the Indian Agent recorded later, "has been a severe blow to the community as he has done good work in many ways." For Elsie that was the understatement of the year. She knew all too well that her husband literally had worn himself out in the service of his people. As she joined her family in the funeral procession leading from her home to the nearby church on Friday, April 20, 1945, she was moved by the tribute being paid to her beloved. Besides their many friends from far and wide, there was a large representation of members of the Canadian Legion from Summerside preceding the funeral party, followed by the school children he had taught on the very day of his death. The twelve pall-bearers (all Micmac Indians) alternated in groups of six as they reverently carried the coffin to the church he had served so well. The Requiem High Mass was celebrated by Reverend J.C. McDonald, Summerside, assisted by Reverend W.V. McDonald, Seven Mile Bay, as deacon and Reverend Urban Gillis, Wellington, as sub-deacon. Reverend Oswald Murphy the parish priest was master of ceremonies. Present in the sanctuary also was Reverend J. A. McDonald from Tignish.

Elsie Sark was indeed paying the price of love as she participated at the Requiem Mass in St. Anne's Mission Church and listened to the *Dies Irae* being sung by the choir her husband had trained. To those who observed her standing at his graveside in solidarity with her devoted family throughout the committal and legion services, she was the valiant woman. As each legionary passed in single file and dropped a poppy in his grave, she and her children whispered their last farewells. They knew in faith that for John J. Sark—beloved husband, devoted father, dedicated teacher, Christian gentleman—life was changed, not taken away. His spirit would live on in them and through them for generations to come.

Martha and Charles Houghton with their three youngest children: centre, Elsie Maud; left, Jack Reuben; back, Ellen Rebecca; c. 1904.

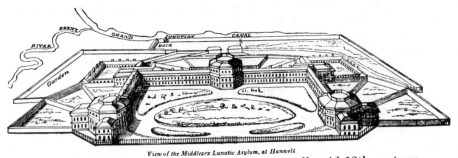

View of the Middlesex Lunatic Asylum, at Hanwell

View of the Middlesex Lunatic Asylum at Hanwell, mid-19th century.
(Courtesy Ealing Public Library)

Elsie Maud Houghton, 1913
(Courtesy Ray Sark)

Wedding Photo: Seated, John J.
Sark and Elsie M. Houghton;
standing, left to right, William C.
Browne, Margaret Dunne, Ellen
(Nellie) R. Houghton and
Joseph Parks.

Postcard portrait, taken in 1915, inscribed on the back "To Darling Jack with all best wishes From yrs with love Elsie." *(Courtesy Ray Sark)*

Group of Prince Edward Island Soldiers from the 24th Battery, D.E.F.O. taken at Moore's Barracks, Folkestone, 1915. Second from the right, Bombardier John J. Sark, N.C.O. *(Courtesy Charlie Sark)*

John Thomas Joseph Sark and
Margaret Thornton Sark (parents
of John J. Sark) *(Courtesy Ray Sark)*

Rev. John A. McDonald, Indian
Agent 1914-1936, Pastor of St.
Patrick's Church, Grand River
and St. Anne's Mission, Lennox
Island, 1904-1936. *(Courtesy E.
Murnaghan)*

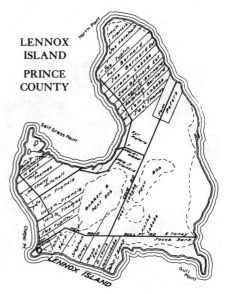

LENNOX
ISLAND

PRINCE
COUNTY

Map of Lennox Island.

John J. Sark, teacher with students at the school. Left to right, from back row to front: Ray Sark, Peter LaBobe, Joan Sark, Madge LaBobe, Joe LaBobe, Jimmy Sark, Elizabeth LaBobe, Mary Iris Sark, Mary Catherine Sark, Jack Sark, Irene LaBobe, Cyrus Sark, Charlie Sark. c. 1939.

Family photo c. 1950. Left to right: Charlie, Rebecca, Joan, Elsie, Ray, Martha and Jack.

Mrs. Sark and Raymond Browne dressed in traditional Micmac costumes, at the Sark farm, October 1948.

Elsie (left) and her sister Nellie on the Lennox Island ferry, 1947.

Elsie Sark with her two oldest daughters, Sister Martha, CND, and Sister Rebecca, CSM, 1972. *(Courtesy John Joe Sark)*

Charlie Sark, 1976.

Ray Sark, in the Handicraft Shop, 1986

Chief Jack Sark in his traditional headdress, 1987. *(Courtesy Anne West)*

Part Three
1945-1973

I have been told all you have done...since your
husband's death, and how you left your own
father and mother and the land where you were
born to come among a people whom you knew
nothing about before you came here. May Yahweh
reward you for what you have done!

The Book of Ruth, II, 11.

12 | New Beginnings

J ohn J. Sark's death marked the end of an era on the Lennox Island Reserve. Twenty-six years had passed since Elsie and John had agreed to remain on the Reserve. They had worked hard in service to the community, and their unusual partnership had sustained them through crises and hardship. Neither of them were accepted whole-heartedly by the Indian community, but this ambivalence appears to have strengthened, rather than weakened their commitment.

The suddenness of John's death had a traumatic effect on the Sark children, especially the two oldest girls. Elsie tried to deal with this during the brief period of time they were on leave from their respective convents and schools; the practical business decisions could wait. As they prayed for the repose of the soul of their Daddy, Elsie reminded them of the text from Scripture which was so familiar to her: "The souls of the righteous are in the hands of God, and there shall no torment touch them." God in His mercy had seen fit to remove their father from this vale of tears. They must accept His will in this as in all things; she herself had long since learned that "in His Will is our peace."

Broken-hearted, Martha returned to her teaching responsibilities in Tignish. One of the pupils who was a boarder at the private school in the early forties recalls that her fascination with the Sark family began at that time:

As a boarder I enjoyed listening to Sister Martha relate stories of her childhood. When her father died of a heart attack, it was a traumatic experience for her. The boarders felt deeply for her. When she returned from the burial she came to the dormitory and told in detail how the Indian p. ople loved him and buried him, made flowers, sang, etc., the whole routine according to their culture.[1]

Rebecca was still a novice with the Sisters of St. Martha; it was necessary for her to return promptly to the Motherhouse in Charlottetown to complete her preparation for religious profession. Ray had another month at Saint Dunstan's and Joan would be in Miscouche until the end of June. Jack and Charlie would be returning to school on the Reserve as soon as a teacher was in place.

It so happened that a month-long search for a qualified teacher proved to be futile, so Raymond Sark was approached to complete the school term. Saint Dunstan's closed on May 18; Ray was ready to take up teaching duties on the twenty-first.

In the meantime Elsie was busy settling her husband's affairs. On June 1 she wrote to the Department of Indian Affairs in Ottawa thanking them for the monetary settlement as well as their kindness and sympathy to her and the children in their bereavement. She concluded her letter with the statement "Should we continue to stay on the Reserve, if there is anything I can do for you, please let me know."

Less than three weeks after her husband's death the war in Europe officially ended; in another three months the fighting in the Pacific terminated with the atomic bombing of Hiroshima and Nagasaki. Before another school term commenced the Second World War was over. Even before the veterans returned home, drastic changes were taking place on the Reserve as a result of recent policies initiated by the Department of Indian Affairs, namely to centralize the Indian population in Nova Scotia and Prince Edward Island on a few large reserves. The rationale behind the new policy was to improve the living conditions and the health of the Indians. To this end, private houses were constructed using Indian labour, paid for from the "welfare appropriation."

In 1945 many people moved back to Lennox Island, but as there was very little steady work on the Reserve, the newcomers were encouraged to farm in a limited way, to produce their own vegetables.

Chickens and pigs were distributed to them as part of the welfare program. As Elsie observed the help which was being handed out, so to speak, she recalled life as it was in the early days:

> The older people were very energetic. They had lovely gardens, vegetable gardens. There were quite a few farms and a lot of stock— horses, cows, pigs; nearly everyone had a pig which they killed in the fall and had their own meat. The land was not good; if they had a stumpy plot where trees had been cut down, they grew beautiful vegetables between the stumps. The old people were grand people; it was a pleasure living with them.[2]

For her part, she realized that without her family's assistance, she would be unable to carry on the farm. The post-war period was a time of new beginnings for her and her family as well as for the Reserve.

Many of the Indians who had moved back had large families, and it was soon evident that one of the most pressing problems was the inadequacy of the schoolhouse. A larger school with at least two classrooms and two teachers was imperative! The response from Ottawa stated politely there was no money for a school! As an interim measure Father Oswald Murphy's mother, Mrs. L.J. Murphy, was hired as schoolteacher. She would be given use of the parish house free of charge with light and heat provided. The children who could not be accommodated in the day school on Lennox Island would be sent to Nova Scotia.

Thus it was that Jack Sark was enroled in the residential school in Shubenacadie, Nova Scotia. He did not leave the Reserve, however, until October 1 because of a polio scare. When Jack left, Charlie was the only child at home for the rest of the 1945-1946 school year. Mrs. Marguerite Maynard remembers Elsie's loneliness that year.

> After Elsie's husband died she came over to our place often, especially in the winter. We lived on the road leading to the Port Hill wharf. She drove a horse and sleigh and tied the horse to a tree while she visited.
>
> Our youngest son was the same age as Charlie. He had a cast on his leg and had to be careful. Elsie and Charlie came over every second day. She brought games for the boys to play with and stayed until 10 or 11 p.m. She was very lonesome when the family was gone.[3]

In the spring of 1946, the Indian Agent again represented to the Department of Indian Affairs the urgent need for a new school on the Reserve. He was informed that "public building had been curtailed in favour of the erection of private homes," and was instructed to send more children to the residential school in Shubenacadie. When school re-opened in the fall, Elsie's youngest son accompanied his brother Jack to Nova Scotia. For the first time, it seemed, Elsie would be all alone, except that Providence arranged otherwise.

While she was visiting the Charlottetown Hospital during the summer she met a Gladys Murnaghan who, after losing a son, was confined to hospital for four months, from May 9 to September 2. According to Mrs. Murnaghan,

> That fall, when Mrs. Sark's two boys, Jack and Charlie, were in Shubenacadie, she offered to come and stay with me as a friend. She came and stayed during the winter and the following spring. While I was convalescing she took care of the house and the children—2 girls and 1 boy. The youngest boy was a year old.
>
> She was a marvellous person, very good to me, my husband Paddy and the children. My children called her "Auntie"—Aunt Elsie. They thought she bossed too much, but she only made them 'mind' as any good mother would. After that she would come back from time to time to help me out when I needed her.

Elsie returned to Lennox Island the following spring to prepare for her sister Nellie's visit.

Before the war the Taylors had contemplated taking a two-year holiday and bringing their teenage sons, Norman and Geoffrey, on a visit to Canada. When war was declared, their hopes were thwarted. In the early stages of the Second World War, in December 1940, Wilfred bought the hardware business on Commercial Road, "Gordon's Totton Limited." Because his was a one-man business, Wilfred was not called into the active armed forces; however, his assistant Mr. Cardey was. Nellie worked side by side with her husband during the war years and put her salary in the bank in anticipation of a post-war visit to Canada. When Mr. Cardey returned from the army and the shop was running smoothly, Nellie was able to make the trip by herself. She travelled first class from Southampton to New York on the SS *America* and then the transcontinental train service in Canada—first to Montreal where she visited her brother Jack, then east to Prince Edward Island to visit

Elsie, and later to Vancouver to visit her brother Charles. The written account of her three-week stay on Prince Edward Island from June 24 until July 16 gives an insight on Elsie's *modus vivendi* two years after her husband's death. The diary also gives some interesting glimpses of Prince Edward Island and its people, Lennox Island and its culture, and the standing of the Sark family in the native and white communities.

Nellie left Montreal on Tuesday, June 24 at 11:30 a.m. She was well satisfied with the lower berth accommodation for the overnight journey to Moncton and, according to her diary, she enjoyed the long, slow jaunt to her destination on Prince Edward Island:

> I changed trains at Moncton and had as company a mother and her three children. As she had made the journey several times before I was lucky to meet her and we travelled together. The train took us right alongside the boat, so we stepped off one onto the other. We sat on the deck and had a very pleasant crossing to Prince Edward Island, about 45 minutes. I landed at a placed called Borden ... The train was again waiting alongside the boat, so it was all very easy. I had to change trains again at Emerald Junction. This was a little local train and had a slow combustion stove in the corner of the carriage for heating purposes in winter.
>
> Prince Edward Island is very clean and very pretty, like the countryside around Bournemouth. The train made frequent stops and took things very comfortable. The journey was interesting as I had an old commercial traveller who insisted on conversation, and as he was deaf, I had the whole carriage an interested audience. He had a wonderful set of gold teeth, every tooth within sight was gold. He said he travelled in fancy goods. He was a scream—must tell you more about him when I get home. Then there was a couple of women, the kind you see in the Yankee films who want to know everyone's business, and one of them shot questions at me at intervals but I gave her answers that got her nowhere.
>
> Then we arrived at the Summerside Station and the old traveller got off. The nosey dame moved up and sat beside me but I diverted the conversation to the local scenery. Then the carriage door opened and a lady dressed in gray burst in and nosey parker said, "Hello, Mrs. Sark. How are you?" Mrs. Sark replied, "Quite well, thanks. I can't stop. I am looking for my sister who is on this train somewhere." So I said, "Don't look any further." Poor Elsie, she got such a surprise as I was sitting next to this nosey parker and, of course, she had not found out who I was and whom I was going to see.
>
> Well, Elsie had a taxi waiting, so instead of finishing the journey on the train we went by car to Port Hill, and a lovely drive it

was—the island is beautiful. It was a long run, cost six pounds or $30.00. Then we had to get into a motor boat and cross to Lennox Island. I was introduced to the ferryman and his mate. When we arrived at the other side, since the tide was rough, we could not pull in, so we had to climb up an iron ladder. It's a short walk from the landing jetty to Elsie's house, past the church along a red pathway. Joan was at home to receive us. Ray had gone to play baseball and was going to a dance afterwards, but he missed the dance and came home to see me instead. He is a nice lad. We all had a nice meal, talk and got off to bed.

On Thursday, June 26, Nellie had an opportunity to tour the island and was favourably impressed by what she saw. She wrote:

Today Elsie and I were talking as it was a wet morning; but after dinner it cleared up and we went for a walk around the island. It is a beautiful little place. There were little houses scattered all around it. There is no traffic, no main roads and the horses gad along the cart tracks, low and gentle. They are building some new houses for the people and soon hope to modernize the whole place. There are as many English-looking people here as Indian and the Indians are dear little things. Everyone speaks English, good English. All are so friendly and think Elsie is a wonderful woman. We are going over on the ferry tonight to walk around the mainland and to post letters. Ray is busy today helping to build the houses and Joan is acting as mother's helper, so Elsie and I have a lot of time together.

Elsie had in store for her sister a variety of sightseeing outings which brought her from one end of the province to the other and included visiting a number of tourist attractions, shopping in Summerside and Charlottetown, meeting Island people and dining in Island homes. The first was a five-day visit to Charlottetown, where Nellie enjoyed a number of visits with Rebecca. It was Nellie's first weekend on Prince Edward Island.

Today we were up early as we were going to Charlottetown for the weekend. Elsie had promised to keep house for friends whom she had spent the winter with. We had to take the motor boat ferry over, and Mr. Daly was waiting with the car and took us up, through Port Hill, a little country road with scattered cottages and farms and long windy country roads that throw off clunks of dust as the car passes along. He took us up to the main road where the bus passes along and waited, but decided to go further to Richmond where we had a chance of bus or train. Here the train crosses the road and

126

people wait there to board it; there is no station or platform. Elsie called on friends, one an 82-year-old lady as active as they make them. We decided to wait for the bus as the trains there are slow.

It was a long ride but pleasant, except in parts where the roads are very dusty and it is difficult to see, and the bus has to slow up considerably. We arrived in Charlottetown about 12:30 and Elsie took me to a very nice café for lunch. The name was Old Spain and it was furnished like the places you see in Spain. It was very unusual and the food was excellent.

The town is like you see in films with sidewalks and grass, no railing in front of the houses. The place we are staying at is an apartment, very nice but nothing like I expected to find after all the talk about the wonderful Canadian apartments and houses. There are three children here. Give me the English kids every time. These kids have no manners and no respect for elders or property. I shall be happy to get back to Elsie's again.

The people we came to stay with left here Sunday morning and are due back on Wednesday morning. We woke early this morning (Sunday) and the folks went to Mass. Then they packed and were out of the house by eleven o'clock. Elsie cooked a good dinner—sirloin roast, peas, beans, potatoes, ice cream, biscuits (cookies to you) and coffee. We had a rest after dinner and then the man's brother called. He had a loan of his brother's car on condition he took us out. So we had a long drive to the shore. It's called Dalvay-by-the-sea. It's a nice place; we drove through a part of the National Park on the way. Here again, the roads throw up clouds of dust. Dalvay is very nice, like Shell Bay, Bournemouth, red soil, lovely sands.

Becky is a nurse in a large hospital here and I spent a couple of hours with her. She is a very nice young woman, very jolly. She is dressed all in white—a nun's clothes when on duty in the hospital. At other times it is black clothes with white around the face. She seems happy in her job and a great favourite with the patients and other sisters. It seems she talked about my visit and all the sisters were anxious to meet Aunt Nellie from England and made a great fuss.

The weather was unusually hot on Monday, so Nellie stayed in the house until evening when she paid Becky another visit. She was taken by the "beautiful, old house" the Sisters had as their home. On Tuesday she wrote,

> Elsie and I went around the shops and saw the town a bit and, once again, called on Becky. The head sister asked us down to supper—high tea. So Elsie got the kids' aunt to come and take over, and

off we went. It was very pleasant as Becky had prepared everything in a little private room, just she, Elsie and I. We had salad, ham, white bread, and butter, saltines, fruit pie and cream, lovely cakes and coffee. It was lovely and beautifully served. We stayed all evening and Becky showed us around the hospital, a lovely place with lots of attention to the patients.

On the return trip to Lennox Island on Thursday, Elsie and Nellie stopped to shop in Summerside. The train did not leave until 6:15 p.m. so they decided to get a taxi home. According to Nellie, "It was nice going across the water on the ferry; everything looked beautiful in the sunshine." She was glad to get back.

There were two major events planned for Monday, July 7, on Lennox Island—the Very Reverend Bishop James Boyle was coming to administer the sacrament of Confirmation and the two Sark Sisters were coming home on a short visit. Everyone was involved in the preparations. Nellie described the highlights in her diary:

There was much excitement on the island today. The Bishop came and confirmed 8 girls and 6 boys. There were great preparations. The lads went into the woods and cut down trees and planted them along the path, both sides making an avenue to the priest's house and across the path used by the priest to the church. Everybody turned out! All work stopped! When the ferry boat left the wharf on the mainland (Port Hill), all the children, choir boys, male choir formed a procession and went to the wharf (Chapel Point) to meet him. When he landed they all started chanting and did so right up to the priest's house. He entered and changed into his vestments—grand affairs they were, too! He had the parish priest and another priest helping him. He looked a real old fellow. I filmed the procession, took a snap. When he walked to the church, everyone followed. I went also. The service is similar to ours. It is a very nice church. The old boy asked to meet me after the service, but I had gone home for a cup of tea.

Later today the girls (Martha and Becky) arrived with the Murnaghan family. Ray and I met them on the mainland. Then we had to start all over again as half the village was there to see them! We went to the house, had a meal and the folks started calling. We finally had a musical evening—a violin, guitar and piano. A tall native played the violin and did it well, stamped his feet in time all the while. Joan played the piano, and Peter, a native boy, the guitar. He also sang his own accompaniment and was good. He works with the CFCY Radio Broadcasting Station in Charlottetown. It was a nice evening. If the room had been larger, I believed we would have danced, but had to be content with just tapping our feet.

The next day it was raining and Nellie was glad as she said it saved a lot of visiting, and she had the girls to herself! When Ray drove Martha back to Tignish that evening, she and Elsie went along. This afforded her an opportunity to see the western part of Prince Edward Island and meet the Sisters at the convent. Again, on Wednesday, when Ray drove Becky back to Charlottetown, Nellie went along. By the time they got to the hospital she noted Becky's "black robes were red with dust from the roads." Ray and Nellie returned by bus; it was a lovely evening and she enjoyed the drive. At Summerside they hired a taxi. "This was also a nice ride," she wrote, "the driver smoking a big Churchill cigar. The moonlight trip over to the island was grand."

Throughout her visit, Nellie received lots of attention from whites and natives alike. The twenty-year-old Ray was exceptionally generous in taking her around the island to meet such relatives as his uncle, Chief Jacob Sark, his aunt Elizabeth Thomas and his cousin Sarah Tuplin. The Indian Agent and his wife arranged a trip to the oyster research station; Father Murphy, his mother and other mainland friends of Elsie had her to their homes for a meal. People like Arthur Francis the ferryman, Bob Strongman from Port Hill, and others did what they could to make her trip a memorable one. On her last Sunday, July 13, Nellie wrote, "I took snaps of all the family and visited folks on the island to say "good-bye." All were sorry that I was leaving."

The day before Nellie's departure, Elsie took her to Charlottetown by bus and arranged a trip around the National Park and, on Wednesday, July 16, accompanied her to Emerald Junction. Why Elsie did not choose to accompany her sister to Montreal and Vancouver is a matter for speculation. Doubtless, she would want to be home on the Reserve while major changes were being effected. She promised her sister that she would take a trip to England, the land of her birth, in the near future. Meantime, there was work to be done on the Reserve.

Part of the plan for the modernization of the Reserve was the construction of a two-roomed school with a teacher's residence, the Indian Agent's residence, a septic tank and outdoor toilets for the school. Elsie, altruistic woman that she was, gave land for some of these official buildings. After postponing the construction for a year, the final outcome of the reconstruction project was a modern four-room school, an agency office and warehouse, an agent's residence and a small nursing station. Eventually a diesel-powered generator was installed to provide electricity for these agency buildings, as well as for the church and the community hall. The Sisters of St. Martha were approached to staff the school and nursing station.

Meanwhile, Elsie was busy arranging the educational future of her own children. Ray was in his last year of high school at St. Dunstan's College and had plans to attend the business college in Summerside the Fall of 1948. This was Joan's last year at the convent school in Miscouche; she would be moving on to Notre Dame Academy in Charlottetown to complete high school. From there she would proceed to Summerside to pursue the commercial course offered there. Jack and Charlie had returned from the residential school in Shubenacadie on June 27 and had made up their minds that they would not return. It was their contention that life was too regimented and discipline too strict at that school; they were even punished, they said, for using their native tongue. Elsie decided to let the two boys complete their elementary schooling on the Reserve even though she knew the schoolteacher Mrs. Murphy was having her problems trying to cope with absenteeism and truancy. Even the provision of the Family Allowance Act regarding school attendance, she mused, had not been effective to date. How her husband had struggled with that perennial problem!

The new school would be in operation in another year; in the interim she would see that her boys did not fall behind in their school work. She would arrange for Jack to take his high school at St. Mary's College, Halifax, Nova Scotia, where he could pursue higher education in Commerce; Charlie she would enrol at the academically prestigious high school in Kinkora in preparation for enrolment at St. Dunstan's College, his father's alma mater. She was determined that each of her children would have the best education available.

During the ceremonies connected with the formal opening of the new school and convent on Lennox Island, Elsie Sark was publicly recognized for her many contributions to the life of the Reserve over the years. The celebrations began with a Solemn High Mass in St. Anne's Church on Sunday, September 12, 1948, conducted by the pastor Reverend E.W. MacInnis, assisted by Rev. J.D. Kelly, Miscouche, as deacon and Rev. Leonard McDonald, Wellington, as sub-deacon. Homilist Bishop James Boyle, who was present in the sanctuary, paid a warm tribute to Mrs. Sark, as repeated in the *Guardian*, the following day,

> In coming as a young English girl to Lennox Island 30 years ago where her environment was so completely foreign to that of her native England, Mrs. Sark had shown qualities of heroism and character possessed to such a degree by few women. Looking back along the years, Mrs. Sark could now say that her sacrifice of ease and the pleasures of her former life had not been in vain. She was now the mother of two Sisters of the Order of St. Martha [sic] and of a son whose academic attainments were much above the average and who, His Excellency felt sure, would give his mother cause for legitimate pride in the days to come.
>
> Mrs. Sark, His Excellency said, had been a means of inspiration to the Indians of Lennox Island and no man could overestimate the benefit which her example had been to those people.

When the new school was officially opened by Lieutenant-Governor J.A. Bernard on the following day, Elsie Sark was once again in the limelight. The ceremonies were presided over by A.E. Arsenault, retired supreme court judge, the man who had taken a great interest in the welfare of the Indians and had sought to promote moves which would better their condition. The occasion, he said, was one of the happiest days of his life—the fulfilment of a nine-year-old dream.

Other speakers were His Excellency Bishop James Boyle, the Honourable G.H. Barbour who represented the Premier, Dr. L.W. Shaw who spoke for the Department of Education, Dr. T.V. Grant, MP, Dr. W.J.P. MacMillan, OBE, and Reverend E.W. McInnis the newly-appointed resident priest of St. Anne's and principal of the new school. The Lieutenant-Governor congratulated the Indians on the progress they were making toward their economic independence and told them that henceforth their boys and girls would be able to secure on their own island such an educational foundation as would enable them to earn their living in any part of the Dominion. The Bishop expressed the hope that the new facility would indeed develop in them "a spirit of self-reliance and independence" and urged them to co-operate with their leaders to achieve this objective. "Efforts made on their behalf in the past," he said, "tended to make them subservient to the government and dependent on it for their livelihood."

Dr. Shaw noted that the school was equipped for both academic and vocational pursuits, referring to the facilities for teaching domestic science and manual training as well as two splendidly equipped rooms for academic instruction. Although his department had no jurisdiction over the school, he said, the provincial Department of Education was willing to share its facilities in any way that might prove helpful. In closing, he remarked that they had recruited in Sister Carmelita Soloman, CSM, one of the best teachers in the province. According to Dr. MacMillan, Sister Mary Magdalen (Connolly), CSM, the new resident nurse, was one of the best the Charlottetown Hospital ever had. He then paid a particularly fine tribute to Mrs. John Sark, "the English girl who came out to the Island with her husband, the late John Sark, after the First Great War and stuck with him and his people, who became the people of her adopted creed and race. It was a demonstration of patriotism and devotion which has been seldom if ever excelled." After the speeches were concluded, the Indian male chorus rendered the national anthem in Micmac and in English. They were clearly Micmacs first and foremost, and their language was alive and well on Lennox Island.

When the formal ceremony was concluded, Elsie was once again in the full glare of publicity. She procured a chief's head-dress and robes which formerly belonged to her father-in-law and put them on the Lieutenant-Governor. The Indians and the whole crowd assembled cheered and applauded while Elsie, Chief Jadis and others posed with him for pictures. Elsie had been accorded a high profile on this occasion by Church and State alike.

Another article in the *Patriot* carried the caption: "New Spirit Evident among the Indians of Lennox Island." The write-up focused not only on the new buildings equipped with modern conveniences and facilities, but also on other recent developments initiated for the betterment of the island, including the planting of 2,500 strawberry plants and 150 fruit trees, as well as the introduction of a pure-bred Ayrshire bull to improve the quality of the new cattle.

Through the co-operation of the provincial government, a number of short courses were given on the Reserve starting in 1948, in the areas of agriculture, nutrition, fishing and community improvements. These new beginnings augured well for the Reserve. Now, professionals were hired to take over the community work that the part-time priest and part-time agent had formerly led, with the help of the Sarks and others.

Elsie was now free to look to her own future, while the Reserve entered a new phase of community development.

13 | A Decision to Stay

It was no secret that Elsie Sark had contemplated leaving the Reserve when her community responsibilities and volunteer activities were taken over by the members of the new regime. She figured that with the rehabilitation of the Micmacs on the Reserve and the provision of essential services—a full-time Indian agent, a part-time doctor, a public health nurse together with a dispensary, a school principal who was also pastor of the St. Anne Mission, a full-time teacher—the stage was set for the establishment of an industrious and contented community. The old order had had its day; it seemed the time had come for her to move on. Jack would graduate from the new Lennox Island Indian Day School at the close of its first year and would be attending the Saint Mary's College High School for boys operated by the Irish Christian Brothers in Halifax, in September; Joan would be continuing her high-school studies as a boarder at Notre Dame Academy in Charlottetown; Charlie would be boarding with the Berrigans in Kinkora while attending high school there; Ray would be working for the Department of Indian Affairs on Lennox Island and would be in a position to assume responsibility for the home and the family while she made a trip to England. It seemed important for her to touch base with her roots before venturing on an uncertain future.

Meanwhile the Indian Affairs Branch of the Department of Mines and Resources had launched its new project on Lennox Island according to schedule, at the beginning of the academic year 1948-1949. Actually housing and school facilities were not ready for occupancy at the time of the official opening, a state of affairs which put a lot of extra pressure on the small pioneer group. In addition to the inconveniences associated with geographic isolation, particularly the frustrations resulting from lack of transport and adequate means of communication, they had to cope with the more immediate problems of housing and heating. The first year of operation proved to be educational in the most basic sense of the word, and the small group of trailblazers were grateful to everyone who understood their plight and came to their rescue. According to Sister Mary Immaculate Loughran, CSM,

> When the Sisters arrived on September 8, 1948, the place was far from being ready for occupancy. The only room furnished was the kitchen. With the help of kind friends, beds were put in classrooms. Mr. MacDonald the contractor gave the Sisters a small table, four chairs and an oil lamp from his workshop. This was the beginning of many acts of kindness on the part of people towards the Sisters, especially on the part of Mrs. John Sark.[1]

The Indians idolized the Sisters and were willing to do anything within their power to assist them. They insisted on sharing with them the first fruits of their crops and livestock, even though the products could have been sold for market gain in Summerside. Joe Tuplin, for example, brought them meat and poultry from his own farm; Mrs. Elizabeth Mitchell gave them milk, eggs, vegetables; others brought berries. To ensure that they would not be frightened by the tramping of the horses running loose at night, two men stood guard near the convent all night long until the Sisters became accustomed to the sounds. During the periods of ice freeze-up and break-up, when travelling to and from the mainland was hazardous, the natives were always ready to assist the Sisters; they even had boards in readiness to cover the holes in the ice. "We were never frightened when the Indians were there," said Sister Mary Magdalen the Superior of the small community of nuns.[2]"They were a great people," she reminisced. When the electric generators went out of commission, they presented the Sisters with a battery radio set.

Not to be outdone in generosity by the Micmac people, Mrs. Sark matched their thoughtfulness in her own inimitable way. Sister Carmelita the primary school teacher recalls with gratitude being invited to Mrs. Sark's home for breakfast the first morning of her sojourn on the island. According to Sister Mary Magdalen the resident nurse, the Sisters had all their meals at the Sark home while their own quarters were being put in readiness. She was a sister of Gladys Murnaghan, so Mrs. Sark left nothing undone to assist her and her companions in their adjustment to the Reserve.

The Sisters for their part were struck by the fact that everyone—government officials as well as residents—went to Mrs. Sark for everything and she did all in her power to help in any way she could. The Indians, they noted, looked upon Mrs. Sark as someone "from away" who was better than they were, who had more and knew more than they did. When, for example, Mrs. Sark's nephew Urban Mitchell was bleeding from a cut incurred while playing hockey, he automatically went to his Aunt Elsie who, he knew, had bandages and everything necessary to remedy the situation. Sister Mary Magdalen herself recalled an instance of Mrs. Sark's kindness when the Mother General of the congregation came to Lennox Island early on, to pay them a visit and size up their living situation. Aware that the stove had not yet been installed in the kitchen, Mrs. Sark appeared at the convent door with a roast-chicken dinner, complete with all the trimmings.

From the Sisters' perspective she was a tremendous person. The Indian appraisal of her, however, was not that clear-cut. On the one hand they sought after her and relied on her services; on the other hand they simply did not trust her. While they fully accepted the Sisters, they merely tolerated Mrs. Sark.

During the first few months, there were frustrations suffered in both the school and the convent because of the lack of heat, light, supplies, and endless interruptions in the daily routine. There had been no requisition for supplies placed the preceding spring, so there were no chairs to sit on and no paper to write on. Sister Carmelita recalls that she was careful to save the envelopes when any of the group received a letter; these were used later for her primary children to write on. The month of October was unusually cold and wet, so when the workmen were unable to get the furnace to work, the new school had to be closed for a month because of the dampness. According to Sister Carmelita, even when the school was in operation, they never had a full day of teaching for weeks at a time because of inspectors, supervisors and other personnel from the department. It was difficult enough, she said, to try to teach English to children who heard nothing but Micmac at home, without having to cope with daily interruptions in the school schedule. Problems with the installation of the generators meant that electricity was not available in the convent, parochial house and the agent's house until December 18. The Sisters managed with a coal stove and oil lamp, but both the priest and the agent were handicapped inasmuch as their houses were equipped with electric stoves! Throughout this period Mrs. Sark proved to be the good samaritan; she seemed to have a ready-made solution for every exigency. She had, for example, a gas iron which she loaned the Sisters for their linens. There was always a good supply of gas in the power house, she assured them.

The practical day-to-day problems encountered in their living and working conditions were more than compensated for by the new spirit that was evident in the community. That fall there was a ready market for the potato basket industry, which was the most profitable source of employment for the inhabitants; a small store was opened, stocked with necessities; and, the best news of all was that of the 111 chest x-rays taken by the mobile unit from the provincial sanatorium in October, only one showed doubtful. Then, too, the leadership offered the youth by Father Emmet MacInnis— the new pastor and school principal—in the areas of religion, sports and dramatics was greatly appreciated. By the time St. Anne's Day rolled around, the 4,000 visitors to Lennox Island had reason to be proud of the great things that were being accomplished on the isolated island.

That summer, when things seemed to be under control on the Reserve and in her own household, Elsie was finally ready to set sail for her native land. Ray recalls that he purchased a one-way ticket for his mother and told her to feel free to stay as long as she wanted to; he would keep the home fires burning. The steamer on which she was to travel, the SS *Aquitania*, was scheduled to sail from Halifax to Southampton, only a short distance from her sister's home in Totton.

Elsie's relatives the Taylors lived in the commercial section of Totton, Southampton. Their apartment was located directly over their ironmonger shop. As a hardware dealer, Wilfred sold locks, tools, pots and pans, paint and china. The effects of the Second World War were still being felt in England in 1949 and it was impossible to purchase new refrigerators and other household equipment. For that reason, a major part of Wilfred's business was repair work; it had grown to the point where he had six assistants. They were kept busy, to Elsie's horror, even on Sundays! She was pleased to learn that the Roman Catholic church of St. Theresa was just across the road from the shop. Here she was able to nourish her faith, so integral a part of her life, by attending Mass and other devotions, now a regular part of her daily activities. This was a dimension of her life in which her sister did not participate.

Nellie accompanied Elsie to London, to Dover and to other familiar places. Elsie was obviously disappointed to find much had changed, especially in London. In Dover, where they remained for several days, Nellie recalled:

> We walked down through the old Market Square to the seafront and along Waterloo Crescent on the right, and then left to East Cliff. A lot of old properties were still standing but the appearance was very different from what used to be. The old officers' quarters were still standing on Guilford Battery. We reminisced there had been three very old cannons on the grounds and two piles of cannon balls which Dad was responsible for keeping clean and tidy. Above was Shaft [Cliffe] Cottage and the old Norman Tower standing on the ground. We climbed the eighty-one steps to the cottage but were unable to enter as it was boarded up. After spending some time there in silence, peering through the windows, Elsie went round to the back. She quietly gathered her own memorial of home: some cuttings of English ivy snipped from the overgrown vines clinging to the white cliffs at the rear of the cottage.[3]

The other cottages which used to be at the far end of East Cliff had been demolished and the old Saint James Cemetery in the centre of the town had been bulldozed to make way for a parking lot! Not only had the town been transformed, but there were very few, if any, friends left. When she was ready to return to Canada, she phoned Ray, according to plan. He crossed over to Port Hill to take the call and assured her that he would send the return fare promptly.

After disembarking in Halifax on the return trip, Elsie visited Jack before continuing her journey to Prince Edward Island. She was glad she had made the trip. The England of her childhood had gone, and she knew in her heart she no longer belonged there. She was more conscious of the fact that she, too, had changed. She eagerly looked forward to returning to the Reserve. Lennox Island, despite its isolation and poverty, was home for her in the fullest sense of the word. She realized the need of maintaining a home for her children on Lennox Island. Here their roots were firmly fixed. It was important that they continue to have a stable base on which to build a sense of belonging. Furthermore, Lennox Island had been home to her for three decades. Being perceived by the natives as a *persona non grata* was of no consequence; she had every right to remain on the Reserve. Remain she would and continue to minister to those in need.

Once Elsie Sark had made up her mind, she proceeded with the practical steps necessary to enhance her living quarters. Over the years her home had been the envy of the native women. Her grand-niece Eleanor Callow recalls the happy days that she as a child enjoyed in her Aunt Elsie's home.

> Her housekeeping was more progressive than that of the other women on Lennox Island. She had a pump in the porch. Everyone had an outhouse, but she had a sink and pump in the porch; that was different. She hung her pots and pans on the wall; no one else did. She had a big kitchen range with a huge warming oven. Every home had an Enterprise stove, but hers was different, probably a different make. Her stove was special in the sense that it had pink enamel and was always immaculate and highly polished. She had a huge kitchen table, big and square. As post-mistress she sorted the mail on that table. (That was the only opportunity I had to see someone working in an official capacity and I was fascinated by the orderliness with which she carried out the task.) I was impressed by the way that she set the table; she always used a pitcher for the milk. She had a buffet made of dark oak with a large mirror; that was different. She had a piano; no one else had a piano. At Christmas time, her tree had coloured metal icicles; no one else had coloured icicles. She had a pantry and seemed to bake more often than other women on the Reserve. I was amazed that she baked bannock as I had associated baking bannock with Indian women. One day when she was baking cookies, I asked her what she was making. I remember her answer: "Fiddle-faddle" and I went home and told my mother. She had peanut butter; no one else had that. I was impressed, even in later years, by the fact that her home was always spotless.[4]

However, now that it was possible to have indoor plumbing— hot running water, bath and toilet facilities—Elsie would not settle for anything less. She did not hesitate to let go of the old house and invest in a new one with all the available modern conveniences. The government had offered to build her a new home in return for the land she had donated for public buildings. Being a business woman, she took advantage of the offer and with the assistance of her son Ray, a new house was promptly constructed on her property a short distance from the original one.

Elsie Sark's progressive thinking extended far beyond the four walls of her own home. She whole-heartedly endorsed the project initiated by the federal government after her husband's death. She believed that improved living conditions and better schooling would benefit the physical, emotional, social and intellectual status of the natives within their own cultural milieu. Furthermore, it was heartening to know that the work she and her husband had tried to accomplish in a limited way on the Reserve, with the slender resources at their disposal, was being carried on, thanks to the largess of the government, to benefit the Micmac people in the entire Atlantic region. She hoped and prayed that the enforced isolation and economic benefits would pay off in the long run, that the natives would eventually emerge with an improved self-concept, equipped to compete with the white population and take their rightful places in Canadian society. She was pleased to point to her own two daughters who had integrated into their respective "white" religious communities, and she was proud of the fact that they were serving Islanders regardless of race or creed through their chosen professions of teaching and nursing. The new program on Lennox Island promised to effect the same for the youth of the Reserve at large and, to that end, she was more than willing to donate her services.

The efforts of the federal government after the Second World War to improve the lot of the Indians on Lennox Island were to have a reverse effect on the Reserve as a whole. There were, to be sure, an impressive number of improvements in housing and physical facilities, as well as new educational facilities and personnel which gave promise of a better future for the natives. The new Indian Act passed in 1951, however, introduced policies that were paternalistic by their very nature and eventually offset the overall gains which apparently had been made. Basically, these policies were directed to the assimilation of the Indians into the larger Canadian society. Some who left the Reserve either lost their Indian identity or experienced a cultural dilemma; others suffered from maladjustment and racist attitudes. Those who remained on the Reserve necessarily became more and more dependent on welfare.

The Band Council that supposedly achieved greater autonomy by the terms of the act was actually stymied from building strong local political institutions.

In the early 1950s, while the government's development plan for the Micmacs was being implemented, Lennox Island attracted a lot of attention from the news media. Mrs. Sark meticulously kept a scrapbook of every news item about the island's success story. There was an atmosphere of optimism, to be sure, as welfare houses were constructed, wells drilled, wharves dredged, new roads built, old roads repaired, new transport and farm equipment provided, oyster beds and blueberry barrens cultivated, pole lines constructed for telephone communications. In May 1953, when receivers were installed in three places—the Agent's office, the store, and the parochial house—for the first time in its history, Lennox Island had direct communications with the mainland of Prince Edward Island. By 1955 electric lighting was available to every home.

No less impressive than the physical improvements were achievements in the academic, social and recreational arenas. School attendance was at an all time high and an ever increasing number of young people proceeded to high school in white communities; a few went beyond secondary school to university or other vocational institutions.

In the case of the Sark children, their mother seems to have had the last word. When, for example, Joan completed the academic high school course at Notre Dame Academy in 1950 and showed no interest in teaching or nursing, her mother registered her in the commercial course offered by the Sisters of Notre Dame in Summerside; when Jack completed high school in Halifax, his mother insisted he register for the university course in Commerce even though he would have preferred to attend his father's alma mater; and, when Charlie completed high school in Kinkora a few years later and expressed an interest in attending the University of New Brunswick in Fredericton, he was offered a scholarship for the freshman year in Science at St. Dunstan's University. This award, established by the Indian Affairs Branch of the Department of Citizenship and Immigration (probably at the instigation of his mother) was given "in recognition of the boy's determination to get an education and his success thus far in doing so; and, to encourage other Indian boys and girls to strive to gain such awards in future and thus to encourage them to further their education." According to Charlie, however, his education was not financed by Indian Affairs because he was not living on the Reserve.

Other educational opportunities were made available on the Reserve for those not bound for university. There were short courses for adults in nutrition, sanitation and recreation. Sister Mary Immaculate recalled how eager the women were to learn.

> One Saturday I remember teaching three women how to make soap. I had saved the grease and bought a can of lye. The following Sunday after Mass they asked if they could see their soap. I cut the large, soft, white block into three parts and gave each one a portion. When they met me later they said, "Sister, that soap is great."

Domestic science and manual training were offered on a small scale for junior high-school students. Sister Mary Immaculate regretted that she had so little time with the girls, only five hours a week.

> The Indian children loved colours. I bought brightly-coloured materials in Summerside and provided needles, thread and thimbles. They sewed beautifully with very fine stitches. Their products were displayed and sold at the Fair at the end of the year. They loved cooking also and were allowed to keep whatever dish they had prepared.

A water-safety program, sponsored by the Junior Red Cross Society, the provincial government and the Women's Institutes of three neighbouring communities was also offered. Red Cross Nurse Evelyn Cudmore recalled that Charlie Sark was enroled in that programme. His mother would have insisted on that!

Various social groups emerged during the 1950s and Mrs. Sark was supportive of each one. Father MacInnis had an active Holy Name Society for men in 1950 and an Altar Boy Society. Mrs. Sark made sure her two boys Jack and Charlie were among the dedicated members of the latter organization. Sister Carmelita recalls that Jack was particularly good around the altar.

There was a Homemaker's Club formed for women in 1952 and a Girl Guide Troop in 1955. Even though none of her immediate family were involved in these organizations, Mrs. Sark took an interest in them and assisted in any way she could. She was involved, too, in the weekly bingo games, the card parties and the dances which were held to help defray expenses on the two new furnaces installed in the church and other worthy causes. She loved to dance and, according to Rebecca, was adept in ballroom dancing. Martha recalls that in earlier times her father would stay home to help her with math while her mother and sister went off to dances.

St. Anne's Day continued to be the greatest social and religious event of the year. In April 1953 the Mother General of the Sisters of Saint Martha presented the Micmac community with the much-coveted relic of St. Anne, and the excitement grew when on July 16 a huge outdoor statue of their patron saint was brought from the mainland by scow; the base had already been put in place on the parochial grounds opposite the church and they were hopeful the statue would arrive for the big day. The maintenance man, accompanied by a contingent of volunteers went "up the Cove" and brought back bushes of lilac. With these they prepared a beautiful shrine. It was against this background that the triduum to St. Anne and the religious services on St. Anne's Day itself took place. Before this outdoor shrine, the pilgrims were seen pleading for favours from their grandmother, good St. Anne. Between the Solemn High Mass at 11 a.m. and Benediction of the Blessed Sacrament at 4 p.m., another area of the spacious grounds featured the activities in which the Indian youth excelled—sports and dramatics.

Under the leadership of Father Emmet MacInnis, the Micmacs quickly developed their athletic capabilities particularly in hockey and baseball. Father had been a hockey star when he attended St. Dunstan's University and had some experience in coaching hockey. With no rink on Lennox Island and very few resources at his disposal—four or five old hockey sticks, a few pair of skates and a puck—he recruited and harnessed the talent of the youth. Despite the fact this his guiding motto was "It matters not whether you win or lose, but how you play the game," success was almost instantaneous. In March 1951 his all-Indian team won the Intermediate "C" Hockey Championship for Prince Edward Island. There was great rejoicing and cries of "Gil Poatm" (We won) in the Crystal Rink in Summerside as Jimmy Hogan, director of physical fitness, handed the trophy to team captain Louis Mitchell. With the addition of an outdoor rink in 1952, thanks to the co-operative efforts of all concerned, there was plenty of opportunity for practice, and in 1953 the Lennox Island team won the Maritime Indian Hockey Championship Crown in North Sydney. Among the consistent players during these years was Elsie Sark's son Ray. A few years later his younger brother Charlie starred with the Island Hockey League. Meantime, friends of Elsie Sark recall how she worried about her boys, especially Charlie when he was at the height of his popularity playing and coaching hockey and baseball in the 1960s.

Baseball was the St. Anne's Day sport which drew large numbers of spectators from the mainland. In October 1951 the Micmac team won the Intermediate "B" Baseball title and were presented with the provincial trophy. For the young men and boys, it was their main interest in summer. When the Tuplin family left Lennox Island in the fall of 1951, their sons were so caught up in the game that they insisted on staying behind on the Reserve until the season was over. So enthusiastic were the Sark boys in the field of sports that it came as no surprise to Mrs. Sark when Jack, in his freshman year at St. Mary's University, in 1952, won the Tom Longboat Trophy as the outstanding athlete in Canada. Less than a decade later, his younger brother Charlie was named the regional Tom Longboat medallist. It was in the 1950s, too, that the Micmacs mourned the loss of Michael Thomas, the king of long-distance runners in the Maritime provinces. Mike was one of them, a Micmac model for such young, outstanding Indian athletes as Barney Francis, Isaac Paul and John Paul.

The Micmacs were no less successful in dramatics. This was an area in which Mrs. Sark was a more willing patroness. Father Mac-Innis had formed a dramatic club in the parish and during the first few years of its existence a series of one-act plays, a comedy, variety concerts and two radio programs were enacted.[5] In 1949 they presented their first one-act play in Tignish; in 1950 they performed in the nearby villages of Palmer Road and Ellerslie on the mainland; in 1951 they brought their shows on the road and staged plays at the Indian reserves of Eskasoni and Shubenacadie in Nova Scotia and the white community of East Bay, Cape Breton Island. Mrs. Sark accompanied the travelling actors and, according to her son Ray, who was one of the actors, she was a good sport as well as a great help. In 1953 the group appeared in seven local communities on Prince Edward Island before full to overcrowded houses. The first radio broadcast, in 1949, presented an all-Indian cast in a 45-minute Rosary Program over the Summerside local radio station (CFCY). During the Marian Year (1954), an all-Indian cast of girls from the Day School were heard over the two radio stations CFCY and CJRW as they presented a forty-minute play entitled "Our Lady of Lourdes." The same year there were variety concerts, one of which was a St. Patrick's Day concert, co-sponsored by Ray Sark and the wife of the Indian agent, in aid of the Hockey Club. Sister

Rita Kinch, CSM, an octogenarian still remembers all twenty stanzas of one song on the program entitled "How the Micmacs Got Their Name," set to the tune of "The Wearing of the Green." With the advent of television on the Reserve late that same year, and the loss of the youth to the high schools on the mainland, stage and radio productions ceased. Displays of talent in the form of dance, music and song by individuals and groups gradually were reserved for the St. Anne's Day celebrations.

The year 1951 was a particularly difficult year all-round for the inhabitants of Lennox Island. The 'flu, which was rampant throughout the province, reached Lennox Island in February. To make matters worse, later that year the new complex of buildings was struck by lightning causing damage to the nursing station. They suffered economically due to potato crop failure, poor fishing and a heavy snowfall which resulted in difficulties in harvesting ash trees. In addition, the usual lucrative smelt run did not materialize. This situation back-fired socially when 35 percent of the able-bodied men migrated to the industrial areas of Canada and to Maine and New England in the United Sates; others joined the armed forces. At one time there were only eight families left on the Reserve.

Frank Jadis was Chief at the time the new Indian Act came into effect on September 4, 1951. When Joe Tuplin—one of the most loved and devoted residents—was forced to leave the Reserve because of the new regulation pertaining to Indian status, the Chief and his councillors were faced with additional problems of an emotional and psychological nature.

Joe Tuplin's parents were white. He was given away by his mother when he was three months old and brought up by three Indian women on Lennox Island. On the Reserve he was known by the name "Bernard" and was accepted as a member of the Micmac community; he had never known any other way of life. He was taught the Indian language before he learned English and became fluent in Micmac. While growing up he did not know the identity of his natural parents. He had a Band number (#12); he voted, and he served as a Band councillor for many years. From his perspective he was one of them, an Indian, and he did not hesitate to marry an Indian woman. He had served in two world wars and, through the Indian Soldier Settlement Act, had acquired property and became a successful farmer. When asked, by federal authorities, to leave the Reserve, he knew from his knowledge of the status of others on the

Reserve that he was given a raw deal.[6] Gentleman that he was, he left with dignity, even though he was told by Judge Arsenault that he did not have to go. Mrs. Sark, who had had a close relationship with Joe since she first came to Lennox Island, was furious; however, she took no action out of respect for his personal wish not to contest the expulsion.

Shortly after the Tuplin family left Lennox Island, Mrs. Sark was faced with a challenge within her own family. Not only had she controlled her children's education, she tried to control their lives as well. Joan had completed the business course in Summerside but there was no job for her on the Reserve. "If you can't make axe handles," her cousin remarked, "Lennox Island is no place for you." Elsie's expectations was that Joan would become a nun. Joan knew she was not called to the religious life, and she had made that clear to all who questioned her on the topic. Moreover, she was determined that her mother was not going to tell her what to do with her life. Joan had a mind of her own. "My mother told me to go my own way in life," she said, "and I did."[7]

Had there been employment on the Reserve her first choice would probably have been to remain there and marry one of her own race, an option her mother would not have appreciated. She spent the summer of 1951 in Eskasoni where Ray was employed with the Department of Indian Affairs. In the fall she went to Montreal where she obtained work, first at St. Patrick's Orphanage and later at other institutions in the city. While working in Montreal she met and married Vincent Beaudin, an Acadian from Miscou Island, New Brunswick, who at the time was a member of the Royal Canadian Air Force (RCAF). Mrs. Sark did not attend the wedding of her daughter which took place in St. Patrick's Roman Catholic Church, Montreal. Whether or not Elsie disapproved of her daughter's marriage is not clear. It seems Vince never visited Lennox Island and some years passed before Joan returned.

While living in Montreal, Joan's only child was born, a daughter whom she named Elizabeth Ann. In 1953, when the baby was fifteen months old, the trio moved to Chatham, New Brunswick. Vince had had his discharge from the air force some time before and was working at St. Mary's Hospital. He had no problem obtaining a transfer to the Hôtel Dieu in Chatham. Although Joan was not in a position to visit Lennox Island for some years, she wrote regularly to her mother and kept her informed of her granddaughter's progress. Actually life for the Beaudins was never easy due to health and economic problems. As a young, conscientious mother Joan would never consider using hard-earned income on the luxury of travel. More than a decade seems to have elapsed before her brothers were successful in persuading her to return to Lennox Island for the St. Anne's Day celebrations. Was Joan, by any chance, sensitive to the fact that by marrying a white man she had lost her Indian status? Was she afraid of having lost face, of being ostracized by her own people? Ironically, it was the outgoing Joan, virtually isolated from home and the family for many years, who had the most positive memories of her mother: "She was always there for us," she said. "She always heard our prayers at night before tucking us into bed. When the time came, she gave me the freedom to go my own way in life."

When Joan left home, the family farm was almost non-existent. True, there were still beautiful flowers and a vegetable garden, but the animals had been gradually phased out after John's death; there was only one horse left. This was the little horse that had been Elsie's almost constant companion for more than two decades. She knew the time had come to make the painful decision to put the animal to rest and, according to Charlie, she did so with dispatch in 1953. She recalled with fondness the time, twenty years before, when the horse had been kicked and maimed, how she did her own veterinary work and nursed her back to perfect health. Now, she mused, she would have to rely on her dog Toodles for companionship!

Mrs. Sark was never idle those years after her family had left home. She continued to be a model of hospitality to all visitors and there were plenty, particularly during the summer months. In August 1951 she enjoyed the company of Dr. Carel van der Merwe, an atomic scientist from New York, his wife, and some of their friends from Prince Edward Island. They were visiting the Reserve during the mammoth regatta which was staged there on August 15. The regatta featured boat races, dory races, the results of the Red Cross Swimming, a boxing card and an evening of outdoor dancing. While Ray took the group on a tour of the facilities on the Reserve, his mother prepared a luncheon for the party in her own home. Then, too, during the year there were the official visitors: the nurses from Indian Health Services, the Regional Superintendent, the auditor, the doctor from Tyne Valley, the school inspector, Mr. Merritt Callaghan, and his wife. Elsie was always ready to meet and greet them. In 1952 when Superintendent Mr. John Kennedy

suffered from amnesia, there was a series of temporary replacements for nine months prior to a permanent appointment, each of
whom needed to be initiated to the Reserve. She never failed them.
Elsie probably was not even aware that her close relationship with
the white Indian agents was deeply resented by the natives. They
disliked authority of any kind, particularly the authority vested in
the agent.

Elsie also endeared herself to the pioneer Sisters who worked on
the Reserve and assisted them also in numerous ways. Sister Mary
Immaculate who was the nurse-in-residence from 1951 until 1960
found Mrs. Sark a tower of strength. "I would go to her for advice,"
Sister said. "She was great security when she voluntarily accompanied me to a home and assisted me in delivering a baby.... I could
not have gotten through the years without her help."[8] In 1954 Sister
summed up her feelings about Mrs. Sark in print: "No pen could
describe or tongue tell the charity and kindness of this woman even
to the present day." In 1958, when Sister Florence McTague and
Sister Rita Kinch were transferred, Mrs. Sark had lost two of her
closest friends. However, she graciously extended the same hospitality to their replacements and had them as guests at her home on
special occasions. It was there, on July 30, 1959, that the Sisters
watched the Royal Visit of Queen Elizabeth and Prince Philip on T.V.

Elsie Sark was a woman who could not relax empty-handed. She
loved to knit in the quiet of her own home. Her grandniece recalled
that she knit socks as did the other women but hers were different;
she knit diamond socks! On one occasion in 1954 while engaged in
this pastime and listening to the radio she answered a question
posed during the program and won the prize—seventy-five dollars.
For fifty dollars she bought a statue of St. Joseph and donated it to
the mission church in thanksgiving for her protection over the years
since her husband's death. With the rest of the money she bought
material for the purpose of replenishing the worn coverings on her
chesterfield set.

There was one point on which all those who knew Mrs. Sark
agreed: by pre-Vatican II standards, she was a dedicated religious
woman. She was a regular attender at Mass and other devotions
and saw that her children lived up to their responsibilities in this
regard. After her husband's death, she continued the practice of the
family rosary in the home and encouraged her friends to do the
same. She smiled when she recalled her husband's response to the
little boy who lost his rosary beads. "The best way to hold on to

them, sonny, is to say them, every day." This dimension of her life was a real asset in a community which placed a high value on religion. When Father MacInnis settled on the Reserve as resident pastor, he had his own housekeeper, so she no longer had the responsibilities connected with the parochial house, the clergy, and the church.

Father MacInnis had a great influence on the young people. He taught them to be reverent in church and kept them involved in community activities. Charlie Sark recalls that Father had May devotions—Rosary and Benediction—every evening during the month, and the altar boys were expected to be present. His cousin John Joe Sark remembers being up at the crack of dawn to collect firewood for the elderly and, lantern in hand, make his way to the church to serve the early morning masses. Religious as she was, Mrs. Sark did not share the warm feelings of the Micmacs toward Father MacInnis in the late 1950s. As a priest she respected him. However, in her opinion, he was a far cry from the beloved Father John A. McDonald, whom she admired and respected during their eighteen years' friendship. She felt that Father MacInnis was altogether too familiar with the Indians, too free with the youth. She made no effort to conceal her opinion that some of his jokes, as well as his actions, were inappropriate for a man in his position in the community.

Mrs. Sark did not like what was happening on the Reserve generally during the late 1950s. Drinking, promiscuity, brawling, vandalism, even violence were rampant. True to character, she did not hesitate to publicly denounce this behaviour, even though she was well aware that the male sector of the population did not appreciate her outspokenness. Her relationship with Chief Jacob Sark had been somewhat distant ever since the rift occurred between their families in her husband's time. She had nothing to lose. Theoretically, she admitted, the new Indian Act of 1951 had given greater autonomy to band councils but in practice, as she saw it, those who had been more or less self-sufficient in the pre-war days were fast becoming more and more dependent on the government. After the Second World War, the Child Allowance Act of 1945 was welcomed as a godsend, inasmuch as it helped to keep children in school, and the Old Age Security Act followed by the Old Age Assistance Act in the early 1950s helped senior citizens maintain their dignity when they were no longer able to work. Now, with the provision of Child Welfare Services by the provincial department in Charlottetown and the Catholic Social Welfare Agencies in Charlottetown and Summerside and a cash system of issuing food assistance to destitute and sick Indians, morale was at an all-time low.

In Elsie's opinion, the government seemed to be encouraging indolence and self-indulgence and, as a group, the Indians were becoming victimized under the new regime. There was little, if any, incentive to work. Potato-basket making was still the most staple industry. The young people took no interest in maintaining the farms. Even able-bodied men were almost completely dependent on handouts. Within a decade, the promise of a brave new world on Lennox Island was crumbling before their very eyes. Elsie was relieved to know that her own sons were gainfully employed off the Reserve. When, in the fall of 1959, she herself was offered the job of housemother at the Stewart House for nurses in Charlottetown, she was elated. For the Sisters of St. Martha left behind to minister on the Reserve, they would miss her encouragement and her helping hands.

14 | Losses and Gains

The darkest decade in the twentieth-century history of Lennox Island was undoubtedly the sixties. Not only did the native community suffer loss of property and leadership during the decade, it was on the very brink of losing its soul.

Ill-fortune for the residents of Lennox Island began with the opening winter. There were several severe storms—one of which in the month of February lasted six days, temporarily depriving the isolated community of electricity and telephone services. The community store and agency sustained considerable damage in a fire. The resident nurse, who had been hospitalized twice the preceding year, had difficulty coping with the various demands on her energies—in the month of January alone, three babies were hospitalized. The lowest point came in March, when Chief Jacob Sark was taken to the Prince County Hospital in Summerside, followed by his death there on May 29, 1960.

There was more bad news for the Micmac community again in the summer, shortly after the St. Anne's Day celebrations, when a forest fire all but destroyed their meagre supply of fuel wood.

Added to this was the concomitant loss of the newly cultivated 350-acre blueberry crop for lack of pickers. Once again, the Indians on the Lennox Island Reserve were faced with the prospect of a bleak winter. It was part of a life-style they had come to accept in silence, without murmur or complaint.

The previous winter, Elsie Sark had enjoyed working as house-mother in the nurses' residence in Charlottetown. The experience was reminiscent of her days at Hanwell Hospital in London forty years before and gave her a new lease on life. Moreover, she was near her daughter Rebecca, who had been employed at the Charlottetown Hospital since receiving her diploma in nursing from the University of Windsor in 1959.

When her friend Gladys Murnaghan requested her services during the winter of 1960-1961, Elsie was delighted. It was an ideal arrangement inasmuch as the Murnaghan home, located on Pownal Street, was just one block from the hospital. She was glad to be in Charlottetown, too, because her youngest son Charlie was registered at the Vocational School there.

Meanwhile, as the Lennox Island residents were silently bearing the strain of community problems, another disappointment was in store when the nursing station was closed at the end of June, 1961, and a decision was made by the Congregation of St. Martha to terminate the services of the Sisters. For Elsie, the withdrawal of the Sisters from Lennox Island, in addition to son Ray's departure on a trans-continental trip, made her consider her alternatives. On the one hand, not one of her three sons had married nor had given any indication of intent to marry. They still needed a home base. She felt, too, it was important to keep the family house on Lennox Island so that her daughters, particularly those in religion, would have a place to stay during their holidays. On the other hand, she was aware that she herself was approaching her seventieth year and conditions on the Reserve not unlike those which prompted the Sisters to leave, made it increasingly unsafe for her to remain in the house alone; her sons forbade her to do so in the winter months. She was visibly annoyed that the new government policy promised so much and yet had brought so little. She was heart-sick at the realization that the good-intentioned efforts of Judge Arsenault had backfired. In the light of what she saw actually happening on Lennox Island, she was taken aback by the decision taken in Ottawa:

> The Joint Committee of the Senate and the House of Commons on Indian Affairs tabled its final report to Parliament on June 8, 1961. After three years of sittings, the Committee agreed that Canadian Indians have made such progress that they will soon be able to

assume the responsibility and accept the benefits of full participation as Canadian citizens.[1]

Her own life's work had made it abundantly clear that no one was more eager than she to rid the Indians of the poor self-image associated with their status as wards of the government; no one more than she wanted to assist them to become full participants in Canadian society. She was disturbed, however, by the paternalistic attitude of the government in their attempts to bring this about.

Director of Indian Affairs H.M. Jones had reported for the fiscal year ending in 1961 that "all the Indian housing needs have been met," that "health standards are high," that Lennox Island is "one of the few reserves in the Maritimes where children coming to school for the first time are all able to speak English." She was perturbed by what he failed to report, namely, that while the Branch's welfare support policy provided all the necessary material benefits for the Indians, it neglected to make any demands for personal and social responsibility in return. Given free education, free medical care, free on-reserve housing for those unable to provide their own, and free welfare payments for food and clothing, what incentive was there for the Indians to work, to help themselves? Marooned on the Reserve and faced with little hope of independence, it was not surprising that welfare cheques were quickly converted into liquor, that alcoholism became the order of the day, that frustrations were countered by vandalism or interpersonal violence. As she saw it, the present state of the Indians on Lennox Island was worse than before.

In response to this situation, Elsie Sark deliberately side-stepped Indian tradition where women were concerned; she moved into the men's world and challenged them to help themselves. She no longer had her husband or the Sisters as sounding boards; she knew the men did not approve of her forwardness, even resented her speaking her mind, but she was past caring. She spoke out loud and clear against the injustices which, in her opinion, were being perpetrated and perpetuated on the Reserve, and she emerged a liberated woman.

As a woman among women on the Reserve in the sixties, Elsie Sark was both admired and resented. Her own great-niece was one of the younger generation who recognized that her Aunt Elsie was aggressive—pushy, bossy, a busybody—but she admired those traits in her. She recalled being at a ball game on Lennox Island one

St. Anne's Day in the early sixties, when her own two children were young, about four and five years of age:

> Aunt Elsie was also watching the game. She came over to where I was standing and said, "I am going home now and I'm taking the children for a nap." She didn't ask, "May I take them?" Simply "I'm taking them." Obviously she was doing me a favour, but she didn't ask. It was her way of helping out.

The same was true in the community at large.

> She was active in church and civic affairs; she had her finger in every pie. If, for example, someone sent ice-cream to the Reserve it had to be eaten at once as there was no refrigeration. Aunt Elsie would be there to scoop the ice-cream and serve it.[2]

Eleanor saw still another dimension of her grand-aunt with which she readily identified: "She loved to talk; she had a great sense of humour; she did outlandish things; she was fun."

Those observations were corroborated by a number of women who were what one might call seasonal friends. Mrs. Sark spent a number of winters in a rooming house for ladies in Charlottetown. "My mother, Mrs. Isidore Smith," said Dr. Catherine Hennessey, "had a guest home for women at 51 Euston Street and Mrs. Sark spent several winters there (at least five) in the early 1960s.... She made for a good spirit among the women."[3] According to one of the guests, Elsie had a bed-sittingroom on the third floor. When Mrs. Smith's health began to fail, meals were no longer available but boarders had kitchen privileges. Mrs. Sark had the reputation of being a grand cook and took over the preparation of the meals voluntarily. Apparently, she made marvellous stew with dumplings. While the food was cooking, she prayed the dish would turn out to her satisfaction. Clare McQuade recalled how they would sit for long periods of time and talk. Elsie would put on the teapot and serve cinnamon rolls for afternoon tea, English-style. "She was very British," said Clare, "the typical British army nurse, the sergeant-major type."

Comments like these indicate she was much loved by the group, especially for her sense of humour.

From the viewpoint of the native women back on the Reserve, however, Elsie Sark was too much in the public eye. They did not appreciate the tributes made her from time to time in the newspapers. When, in the winter of 1961, she was interviewed by Mrs.

154

Helen MacDonald for a CFCY Radio program, they questioned why she was chosen instead of one of the Micmac or French-Acadian women who served the Reserve well. When she was honoured later by a judge of the Supreme Court with a Canadian Club award for her work among the Micmacs, her colleagues were not even aware of it. Despite her seemingly haughty manner, Elsie was a very modest woman and each of these recognitions was taken in stride. She accepted each one graciously, but there was no gloating over any one of them. She did not even mention them in her letters to her sister. According to Nellie, "Elsie was never a person to talk about her life and her accomplishments. She just went through life doing good."

Meanwhile, Nellie and her husband Wilfred planned a trip to Canada in 1962. So, when the ferries were running smoothly in late spring, Elsie returned to Lennox Island to get her new home, complete with indoor plumbing, electricity, prepared for the Taylors. She had just received her first Old Age Security cheque from National Health and Welfare!

Once on Prince Edward Island, the Taylors had the use of nephew Charlie's brand new Ford Console car, which enabled them to travel extensively and capture the Island's beauty on film: the red soil along the Lucy Maud Montgomery-Anne of Green Gables tour route, the sand dunes at Cavendish beach, the beautiful farm houses scattered throughout the island—"not a shabby one among them"—and the Lennox Island skyline with its impressive church spire as viewed from the wharf on the Port Hill side.

In Ray's absence, Jack took over as tour guide. His aunt and uncle were spellbound by the beautiful potato fields and fascinated by the potato beetle which Jack carefully brought to their attention. They saw the fishing facilities and had a close-up view of oyster beds and lobster traps. During the time of their visit, Kinkora was still Charlie's headquarters. The Berrigan home was still his "home away from home." Maurice and Kathleen had provided Charlie a home ever since his high-school days.

After a ball game one evening he took time out to go to Lennox Island in a friend's car. It happened to be his first date with Doreen Simpson who was holidaying on Prince Edward Island, so he was not too happy having to give up his car while the Taylors were visiting. To make matters worse, Will "smashed the car!" His uncle wanted to pay for the damage but, much to Charlie's chagrin, his mother wouldn't hear of it! Doreen smiles when she recalls that first visit to the Sark home. She felt she was being scrutinized and found wanting!

In 1964 Elsie returned the Taylors' visit with a trip to England, herself. This was but one of the many highlights in Elsie Sark's life in the mid-sixties. These were the years for family celebration and travel, and she thanked God that she had the health and the freedom to enjoy these experiences. There were the marriages of her three sons within the short span of two years; the birth of her first grandson; and, the many invitations and opportunities to travel within the Maritime provinces and beyond, especially to the United States.

Jack was the first of the boys to marry. At the time he was an assessor for the income tax department in Charlottetown. His fiancée Marilyn Francis, a graduate of Mount Saint Vincent University in Halifax, was a clinical and surgical instructor in the Hillsborough and Charlottetown hospitals. She was born on Lennox Island, the daughter of John Andrew and Emma (Gallant) Francis. Their marriage in St. Anne's Church, Lennox Island, one week prior to St. Anne's Day, 1964, was the last wedding over which Father Emmet MacInnis presided. Marilyn, now a public health nurse for well over a decade, summed up succinctly her perception of Mrs. Sark's attitude in the sixties: "Can anything of good come from Lennox Island." In Elsie's opinion Jack could have done much better; however, if he chose someone from Lennox Island as his wife, Marilyn was as good, perhaps, as could be expected! Jack had never been particularly close to his mother. As a thirty-year-old business man, he was well able to make his own decisions. Actually, over the years, Marilyn enjoyed a good relationship with her mother-in-law, particularly from the time her first child, a son, was born. "She was fortunate," she said, "we lived a good distance from Lennox Island."

Elsie's oldest son Ray was next. He had had a serious heart attack while vacationing on Prince Edward Island in the summer of 1965; but, thanks to Kathleen (Donnelly) Berrigan, he survived. When therefore he returned to his job in finance and real estate in California, he was a source of constant worry for his mother until he, too, married in January, 1966. She even went to California to be with him! His fiancée Frances Reid, daughter of Walter and May (Cullen) Reid from Hope River, Prince Edward Island, was teaching school and studying at Sacramento State University at the time. Their marriage was solemnized in the Church of St. Joseph, Marysville, with Father Anthony Traynor presiding. Ray could do no wrong in his mother's eyes, so there was no question about Fran's acceptance into the family. As a matter of fact, Mrs. Sark spent two winters with the couple in California before her death.

Charlie Sark and his fiancée, Doreen Simpson from Staten Island, New York, had announced their marriage for the month of August of the same year. Charlie was still living with the Berrigans in Kinkora; he was employed as an electrical engineer by CN Marine in nearby Borden. From the time she was a child, Doreen spent her summer holidays with her grandmother in Travellers Rest. That summer, while working in Summerside, she was boarding with her uncle, Alex MacDonald. Thus, they were married in St. Paul's Roman Catholic Church in Summerside. The charismatic Father Gerard Tingley, whom Charlie had come to appreciate at St. Dunstan's, was celebrant of the Nuptial Mass. Doreen recalls there were a lot of raised eyebrows as the ceremony proceeded in post-Vatican II style.

This wedding was the occasion for a great family celebration. Ray and Fran came from California; Jack and Marilyn brought their son Darcy; Joan was there with Betty Ann. From that point on, the two grandchildren seem to have been the focus of Elsie's attention. She is reputed to have become more loving and friendly and was heard boasting about her grandchildren.

When all her children were well settled, Mrs. Sark capitalized upon the many invitations and opportunities to travel, visiting her family and her friends. She spent two winters, for example, with Ray and Fran in California, one in Marysville, one in Sacramento. Her previous visit to California in 1961 had been by train. Ray remembers taking her up Mt. Shasta, to Oroville—the largest earth-filled dam—to the town where she boarded the train for home. He has pictures of her taken in Disney Land, the Italian Swiss Colony, in the winery at Santa Rosa, next to a tree in Chico. Her later trips were by plane. Both Fran and Ray recall driving her to San Francisco and having a pre-flight cocktail with her at the Mark Hopkins or Fairmount Hotel; she took back the swivel sticks as a souvenir of that event! Fran has pleasant memories of her mother-in-law's visits. "She was a great sport, loved to attend social functions, to go out to dinner and dances; she was always at ease and well-accepted as one of the group; she was always well-dressed, adorned with pearls; she had a hearty laugh."

Ray recalls that he was active as a fourth-degree Knight of Columbus at the time, and his mother accompanied Fran and himself to the various social functions associated with Council #953, such as the induction of the Grand Knights, dinners and socials for women at the chapter meetings.

Then, there was a time she went to New York by car to spend Christmas with Charlie and Doreen at the Simpson home on Staten Island. Doreen's grandmother, Mrs. Dan MacDonald from Travelers Rest, sat in the back seat with Mrs. Sark, while Charlie at the wheel and Doreen as navigator by his side made their way through a blinding snowstorm in December 1968. The couple smile as they recall that the only sound that could be heard from the rear of the car was the rattling of rosary beads! Becky, who was stationed at Newark, New Jersey, at the time, was there also for the holiday season. After New Year's the two elders flew to California, Mrs. MacDonald to visit her daughter Mary, Mrs. Sark, her son Ray.

It was during those years, too, that Mrs. Sark made visits to friends and relatives in Boston, among them Irene LaBobe and Eleanor Callow. Mrs. Bessie MacNeil from Tyne Valley remembers the time Mrs. Sark appeared at her home in a dress purchased in Boston. "It was identical to one I had bought in Boston that same year," she said. Then there were the regular visits to Martha in New Glasgow, Nova Scotia; to Joan in Chatham, New Brunswick; and, to Tignish, Prince Edward Island, when in 1967 Jack accepted a position as assistant manager of fisheries, and moved his family there.

This was a different kind of experience! Shortly after Jack and Marilyn were settled in their new home, they became instant parents of three more boys—the Gallant brothers—who had been placed in foster homes after their parents had a car accident. Their father was killed in the accident and their mother sustained serious injuries which necessitated hospitalization for some time. Peter was only seven months old when Social Services placed him in their home in March; Michael was eight years old when the Sarks took him in May of the same year; and Larry was five years old when he joined his two brothers in July. Less than a year later, while Elsie was celebrating her seventy-seventh birthday in California on April 1, 1969, she learned that Marilyn had given birth to another son, Kevin—another grandson. By this time, Michael had returned to his relatives; Marilyn and Jack now had their full family, four boys.

Meanwhile, things were going from bad to worse on the Reserve. In the final report of a fifteen-month study conducted by anthropologist Frederic J. Gross, of St. Dunstan's University, dated July 1969, the author presented "a statement of what would be needed for the Lennox Island community to transcend its present status as a perpetually poverty-stricken refuge almost totally dependent for its very existence and survival upon the generosity and good graces of Her Majesty's Government."[4]

Actually the Micmacs themselves were well aware of the status quo and had been attempting for the past few years to cut through the political red tape to alter the so-called "poverty-welfare cycle." When, for example, James Sark (Jimmy) returned to Lennox Island in 1965 after an absence of five years, he was appalled by what he saw. "The place was a mess," he admitted.

> No one was working; everyone was on welfare. There had not been a new house built since the mid-fifties; the farms had disappeared; there had not been a St. Anne's Day celebration in five years; the church was in bad shape; the school was even worse—not only was there a constant turnover in teachers, but those who were hired were not perceived as good role models and therefore did not have the respect of the pupils; one female teacher, he was told, kept a shotgun on her desk at all times![5]

When he was elected Chief the following year there was much to be done and he was determined to put his youth, intelligence and energy in the service of his people. Housing and other necessities for survival on the isolated island were priorities and he began by arranging for houses to be built, providing a store stocked with the essentials, purchasing refrigerators and washing machines, continuing work on the pipeline which had been started in 1961 for the purpose of providing domestic water supply for all the residents on the Reserve. Meanwhile, on January 1, 1966, the control and supervision of Indian Affairs was transferred from the Minister of Citizenship and Immigration to the Minister of Northern Affairs and Natural Resources. This change meant more hurdles for the enthusiastic young Chief.

As hope was being restored on the Reserve, the natives were saddened by the news of the sudden death of the priest who had lived among them and ministered to them over the past nineteen years. Father Emmet MacInnis died at his family home in St. Peters early in April, 1967; he was just fifty-two years old. Father had been

159

on sick leave for about three weeks. He had resigned from the parish and school, and was travelling back and forth to St. Peters where he was building a cottage at Cable Head for his forthcoming retirement. The Chief recalled, "He used to stop at my home for tea on his return to Lennox Island from St. Peters. The evening he did not return, I distinctly heard his knock on the door." John Joe Sark, who had returned from Boston in February, recalled with sadness that he accompanied Father across the ice the day he left and did not return. "I remember helping him to tie his snowshoes that day," said John Joe.

The entire community of Micmacs loved Father MacInnis, understood his alcohol-related problems, empathized with him during his periods of loneliness and frustration. All those who were able to make the trip across Prince Edward Island to attend the funeral Mass, St. Peter's Church, April 6, 1967, did so. Among the active pallbearers were Chief James Sark and Councillor Joseph LaBobe. The natives in the congregation knew in their hearts that their deceased pastor and friend would have taken exception to homilist the Right Reverend Dr. J.P.E. O'Hanley's description of them as "a simple, unlettered, and too often indolent congregation," but they agreed with the statement that "Father MacInnis displayed an extraordinary spirit of gentleness and of humility" as he provided pastoral care to a deprived people in a depressed area.[6]

Mrs. Sarah Tuplin summed up the sentiments of the community well: "The Micmacs were his people; they loved him; they wished he could have been with them longer."

While they were still mourning his loss, the bishop asked Father John Cash, the pastor of St. Patrick's parish, Grand River, to assume responsibility for the St. Anne Mission. Father Cash proved to be the right person at the right time!

Once a new spiritual leader was in place, Chief Sark in collaboration with him moved on to the next item on his agenda—education. He formed a committee of three to look into the possibility of having the Sisters of St. Martha return to the Reserve. Accordingly, the trio—Mrs. Emma Francis, ex-chief Ray Lewis and Chief James Sark—approached Mother Mary Angela Keefe, the Mother General of the Congregation and presented their request. So impressed was Mother Angela and her council with the sincerity of the appeal made by the natives themselves that they stretched their personnel to the limit and reopened the Lennox Island foundation in the fall of 1968.

Before Mrs. Sark left for the United States that winter, she was heartened by events in Canada, in general, and on the Lennox Island Reserve, in particular. The newly elected Prime Minister Pierre Elliot Trudeau was determined to create a just society, and his newly-appointed Minister of Indian Affairs and Northern Development, Jean Chrétien, gave promise of better days for Canada's Indians. With a promise of a brighter future for the community on Lennox Island, Elsie looked forward to returning after ice break-up in the spring.

15 | Resigned to God's Will

Elsie Sark returned to Lennox Island in May, as was her custom, to open up the house and settle down once again for the summer months. During the fall and winter (1968-1969) she had enjoyed six months of travel and entertainment in the company of her children, and she was looking forward to a quiet and peaceful summer among neighbours and friends. She had plans, too, to spend the upcoming winter on the Reserve, something she had not done for over a decade.

When she arrived on the Reserve there was an unusual amount of hustle and bustle. As usual, she made it her business to find out what was going on. On March 17, Premier Alex Campbell had signed a 725 million-dollar agreement with the federal government covering a fifteen-year comprehensive development plan for Prince Edward Island. The plan had an overall purpose to improve the productivity of the Island province. This would be achieved by finding and developing new markets, as well as better means of reaching those markets. Lennox Island was to be an integral part of the plan:

> It is the intent of the agreement that the members of the Lennox Island band be eligible to receive all Plan benefits. To this end, the Province of Prince Edward Island will take early steps to conclude an agreement with the Minister of Indian Affairs and Northern

Development on administrative and jurisdictional questions, so as to avoid any delay in implementing the provisions of the Plan.[1]

Two non-Indians had already been hired to work on the Reserve: one, Mr. Louis Pellissier, was given a part-time position to offer upgrading courses and to assist with the organization of Manpower-sponsored programs; the other, Mr. Angus MacIntyre, a full-time community worker position with responsibilities relating to all the Reserves on Prince Edward Island.

The young Chief and his Council were not too happy that these men were hired before there was adequate input from the Band. The Band leadership, she learned, was particularly upset because of the consequences of the government's "well-intentioned" moves. A large percentage of the adult population enroled in the upgrading and retraining programs, for which they were paid far in excess of what their welfare checks would have totalled. This increase in immediate cash meant more alcohol, more fighting and more vandalism in the small community. She was sad to learn that conditions were such that the women were asking for full-time protection from the Royal Canadian Mounted Police (RCMP). She would give the women the moral support they needed.

Before long it became clear to Elsie that the unrest among the Indians was not limited to the Micmacs on the Lennox Island Reserve. Those living in the Scotchfort and Morell Reserves had already petitioned the Indian Affairs Branch to establish them as a band separate from Lennox Island. On the Canadian scene Harold Cardinal's recently-published book, *The Unjust Society: the Tragedy of Canadian Indians*, denounced the new government policy tabled in the Commons in June.[2] She had personally agreed with the federal-provincial objective to terminate special status for Indians and to work toward the full and non-discriminatory participation of Indians in Canadian society. It was what she herself had in mind for her own children; yet, the Indians, nationwide, were not prepared to discuss the White Paper until the question of land claims was settled.

Meanwhile, Elsie was preoccupied with the practical business of running her own life, getting her house in order, renewing old friendships, attending to her health needs. She was satisfied that her young nephew was looking after the affairs of the Reserve. Jimmy Sark, for his part, has vivid memories of his Aunt Elsie. "She never interfered with me or my work," he said.

She went from her house to the store, to the wharf, to the church, to the hall. She minded her own business. She was friendly, would talk with anyone. She didn't deliberately step on people's toes, but if asked a question she didn't beat about the bush. She didn't mind giving her opinion on any issue and she did so in a frank and forthright manner.[3]

The Chief recalled with amusement the time his aunt came into the store and began sniffing in an audible way. "It smells stale in here," she remarked. "I wasn't aware of it until you came in," her nephew retorted. They both laughed. For Elsie, this was a new generation indeed!

During the summer of 1969, Elsie enjoyed the company of her next-door neighbour, Angie Mathers. Angelina was only fourteen years of age when Elsie came to Lennox Island in 1918. Her mother had died when she was only seven, and she experienced what she called "a terrible childhood."

I left home when I was fifteen years of age. I did not want to live there. I could only get three cents a quart for blueberries and I resented the fact that I could barely speak English, that I had no education, that all I could do was wash dishes and scrub floors.[4]

Fortunately, Angie had a good time working for a family in Spring-hill, Nova Scotia, for $5.00 a month. Later she went to the United States to work, married an American and remained there until her husband's death forty-two years later. She was then sixty-five years of age and decided to retire to her native land. Once there, she learned to her disgust that the government policy relating to non-status Indians would not permit her to settle on Lennox Island permanently. She was given temporary living quarters in the government house until she was able to find a suitable place. She was there until after Elsie's death when Ray helped her settle at Rocky Point, not far from the Indian Reserve. Speaking of Mrs. Sark, "She was my dear friend to the last day," said Angie. "I loved the woman as a friend and was broken-hearted when she was gone."

Elsie and I would go to Summerside, have dinner together, go to the beauty parlour to have our hair done, go to the Linkletter Motel for the night, have breakfast together, finish our shopping and take a taxi home... Sometimes I would cook something extra (she didn't bother), go to the window, call her and tell her that dinner was on the table. At other times I would go to her house and she would make tea and cookies. In the evenings we would go for a short walk to the wharf. We went to church together—she was a much better Catholic than I was! We would play cards all afternoon; we would try to see who would get solitaire first!

That fall, after surgery, Elsie was faced with the dreaded verdict of cancer! Once again she bowed before the will of God and eventually heeded the advice of her youngest son Charlie. She had followed his advice a year ago before going to New York and, with the assistance of barrister Bernard McCabe of Summerside, she had made up her will. Rebecca was still stationed in New Jersey, so she was pleased that Martha was permitted to come from New Glasgow to be with her during convalescence. Charlie had boarded up the house on Lennox Island and would not hear of their staying there during the winter months. Elsie, for her part, would not tolerate Martha being away from her teaching responsibilities for more than three weeks. When, therefore, Elsie was released from hospital, Charlie brought both Sister Martha and his mother to his home in Kinkora. At the time, his wife Doreen was in the Prince County Hospital giving birth to their first born child—a baby girl. After the baby was christened Sarah, and the celebrations were over, Charlie found a suitable apartment for his mother in Charlottetown. There she would be close to the hospital where she was scheduled to go periodically for treatment. Martha returned to New Glasgow.

In the spring of 1970 there was evidence of new life on the Reserve. The Sisters were completing their second year in the school, under the leadership of Sister Christine Doyle, a relatively young woman who was in tune with the times and sympathetic towards the youth of the sixties in general, and the Indian youth, in particular. She appreciated the fact that in John J. Sark's day, when Micmac was the dominant language on the Reserve, the school was the great transmitter of Micmac culture. Over the past quarter century, however, schooling along the lines of the provincial school curriculum was an exercise in futility on the part of teachers and pupils alike.

Rapid changes were taking place under the aegis of the comprehensive development plan, including a shift of responsibility from the Regional Office in Amherst to the Band itself. This change in political structure paved the way for initiative to be exercised on the local level. As a team, the Chief, the Council, the pastor, the school principal and staff and the nurse lost no time planning for the amelioration of conditions on the Reserve. A so-called ecological approach to education was designed and espoused which embraced every facet of the culture—schooling, religion, community development, law enforcement, health care, political growth, recreation, transportation and beautification. The focus was to be on "the person," the main objectives being the building of self-worth within a people who had lost their spirit and saw themselves as inferior and the restoration of the Indian identity of a once proud race.

This approach required a concentration on Indian culture and was accomplished through the use of resources latent within the Reserve. To quote from Sister Christine:

> From the community we were able to find people to teach leather tooling, basket-making, beadwork and such crafts. The Micmac language became a regular part of the curriculum. Native songs and dances received special emphasis in the music program. Indian people served in various capacities within the school—school councillor, teacher aide, language teacher, craft instruction.[5]

From Sister's perspective, the role of the religious at Lennox Island went far beyond being a good administrator and teacher. "It extends," she said, "to reaching the inner core of a wounded people to restore light, hope and peace for them."

Elsie Sark had no problem relating to this praiseworthy goal; it was the process through which it was to be achieved that bothered her. Things were changing indeed; it was not like the old days! A generation gap had emerged, to be sure. She was experiencing the beginning of another cycle in the evolution of Lennox Island, a "third wave," so to speak, one in which she would not be actively involved.

Elsie spent a peaceful and uneventful winter in an apartment in Charlottetown. The following spring brought the birth of another grandson. On the April 30, 1971, Charles Gregory was born to Charlie and Doreen. The rejoicing was interrupted the following day—Sunday, May 1—when word spread that, for no apparent reason, the two-room school and convent had been completely destroyed by fire while the Sisters as a group were on the mainland. This was to be but the first in a series of disruptions and intimidating experiences for the residents of the Reserve that year.

The inconveniences borne by the Sisters for the two months prior to the closing of school in June were compounded in the fall when, the day after classes were resumed, the Lennox Island ferry, a forty-foot vessel, suffered the same fate as the school and convent four months previously. The Sisters had been commuting from the parochial house in Grand River as their new convent would not be ready until November. There was no adequate replacement at hand for public transportation to the mainland, so the Chief had no choice but to hire a boat from the white community. It was this action which allegedly gave rise to the traumatic experience which was to shock the Reserve two months later, an experience from which Mrs. Sark was mercifully spared.

On Wednesday, November 10, Elsie Sark was taken to the Prince County Hospital in Summerside after suffering a slight heart attack. This was followed by a massive attack the next day, Armistice Day, after which her name was entered on the critical list. When notified of their mother's condition, the entire family including Ray from California came home. As her three sons and three daughters assembled at her bedside, they knew intuitively that in this, as in all the trials and sufferings of her life, their mother had resigned herself to the will of God. When, therefore, they witnessed her miraculous recovery and release from hospital, they knew that the spirit of life had not given up in her.

While Elsie Sark was still a patient in the Summerside hospital, a serious disturbance erupted on Lennox Island which continued for three days. It entailed death threats to individuals and intimidating phone calls to their families. The RCMP were called to the scene and arrests made. It was a disturbance which no living witness is willing to recall or is prepared to discuss, a disturbance nevertheless which had far-reaching consequences. According to the newspaper accounts, the trouble arose over the hiring of a white man to work on the ferry when there was a high rate of unemployment among the natives.[6] Actually the source of the trouble was complex and incomprehensible to anyone who was not involved in the community. There was nothing to do on the Reserve from sun-up until sun-down. "It was bad enough being an Indian in those days," said Father Cash, "without the isolation factor."

From her hospital bed Elsie learned of the goings-on on the Reserve. How she empathized in spirit with the older people who had no alternative but to stay! God knows that she herself had been through many a similar episode in her life. She, too, was convinced that isolation was the root cause of most of the Reserve problems, inasmuch as it engendered feelings of distrust toward the white community and frustrations among themselves born of jealousy. Fighting and quarrelling were a natural release. She was sad to learn that the Chief together with Councillor Arthur Francis had left Lennox Island and were in the process of setting up the Band Office in the federal building in Summerside. There were rumours and there was gossip about the Chief's personal life and grumblings about his dictator-like leadership, his unsatisfactory use of project funds etc? It was an old familiar story. She was glad that Becky had invited Martha and herself to the Sacred Heart Home in Charlottetown for the Christmas holidays. She would not have to return to the Reserve under these depressing circumstances.

In January, Elsie had to be hospitalized once again. This time, Becky arranged for her mother to have the use of her room in the convent area of the Sacred Heart Home after her discharge from the hospital. There she remained for the rest of the winter. Still alert to news from the Reserve, she knew the Micmacs resented the removal of the Band Office and were in the process of signing a petition to have it returned to Lennox Island.

She was surprised that Chief Jimmy Sark—now a *persona non grata* on Lennox Island—was arguing against the proposed causeway-bridge on the grounds there were not enough people to justify the million-dollar project. She had always respected the young Chief's judgment; however, on this point she was a conscientious objector. She was convinced that Lennox Island had no future without a fixed link with the mainland and she would write to the provincial premier to underscore her position.

She was also aware of a referendum being taken to determine whether the Indians of Prince Edward Island wanted one or two Bands. The majority of respondents opted for two. Approval of the decision was sought from Ottawa and obtained. Thus, after four years of negotiations with federal authorities, the separation of the Lennox Island and Scotchfort (later known as the Abegweit Band) bands became a *fait accompli.*

When the first election took place on May 9 for the position of Chief on Lennox Island, Mrs. Sark's son Jack was elected by acclamation. Sister Mary Immaculate was the first to congratulate Mrs. Sark. "She was not happy," Sister commented. "She felt there was too much responsibility."

When the unrest and excitement subsided, Elsie Sark returned to her island home to spend another summer among friends, and she was not disappointed. Work on the connecting link with the mainland had been delayed one whole month due to bad weather and a late spring. She was well satisfied, however, that the two governments had agreed to go ahead with the project, proud that its realization was "due in no small measure to the persistence and determination of Chief Jack Sark."

In anticipation of its completion in the fall, she bought a new car to enable Becky to travel to Lennox Island on her day off and do her errands. There were more delays when the materials for the bridge did not arrive on schedule. November proved to be an unrealistic date for completion; it would take an additional few months. An impressive ceremony was being planned for the official opening which would fittingly take place on the feast of St. Anne. As the oldest resident, she might have expected to be honoured as the ribbon-cutter.

Meanwhile Elsie Sark and Angie Mathers were close neighbours and solicitious about each other's welfare. They agreed if the curtains were not opened in either of their residences at a reasonable hour they would check on one another. When Angie noted that Elsie was not up and about as usual on Thursday morning April 12, she went next door to visit her.

"She was lying on the couch, fully dressed with her boots on. She hardly spoke," said Angie.

Angie left to do an errand for her as Becky providentially arrived. Later, while driving across the new causeway-bridge en route to the hospital, Mrs. Sark requested her daughter to stop while she offered a prayer of thanksgiving to God. She had lived to see the road to the liberation of the Micmacs on Lennox Island.

Elsie Sark rested comfortably in the intensive-care ward throughout the first few days of her hospitalization, with Becky at her side, constantly. On Wednesday, Becky noted a change in her mother's expression. Quickly and quietly she slipped out of the room to alert her brother Charlie to the situation. Within minutes, Elsie had slipped away, peacefully, to her eternal reward.

Elsie Sark's death and burial notices were carried in the local papers on Holy Thursday. Those who knew this valiant woman and read the accounts agreed that it was fitting indeed that a life which was symbolized by the cross should terminate during the week which liturgically coincided with the passion and death of the

Lord and Saviour, and that the funeral Mass on Easter Monday should be that of the Resurrection. The obituary appeared in the local papers on May 10 and paid tribute to "one of the province's noblest and much-loved women."[7]

Although she, herself, did not live long enough to participate in the christening ceremony of the crossing named Ulnoo Asomlgan, the satisfaction of knowing that Lennox Island would now have an open road to the rest of the world, released her from her lifetime of service.

Afterword

At the formal opening of the causeway-bridge three months after Elsie Sark's death, staff-writer for the *Journal-Pioneer* observed, "In reality the causeway does represent a pact between two races and will hopefully promote a better understanding between them." It is significant that Jack Sark presided over those ceremonies as Chief of the Lennox Island Band of Micmac Indians—as son of Elsie and John Sark.

The Sark children learned to straddle two cultures from a very early age. Born of mixed-race marriage, brought up on the Lennox Island Reserve, they were always in the midst of political tensions. Their parents ensured that they had access to the educational opportunities and life-style enjoyed by middle-class white children living on the mainland of Prince Edward Island. Having lost their father relatively early in life, they were naturally influenced by their mother's view of life and attempted with no small measure of success to live up to her expectations. Elsie's influences rooted in the Protestant ethic of hard work and high moral standards were as strong as, if not stronger than the day-to-day ambience of the lackadaisical, warm, easy-going atmosphere of the Indian community.

When she was gone, without her support, they were faced with the reality of their own existence, of who they were. Their problem was compounded by the fact that the native peoples of Canada recently had found a common voice in the National Indian Brotherhood (now called the Assembly of First Nations) and had attracted political attention in their demands for educational reform and the restoration of aboriginal rights.

This turned out to be a critical turning point in their lives. Having led relatively sheltered lives in white neighborhoods for a quarter of a century, the new climate would have given the Sark daughters cause to reflect on their own cultural identities. Martha, for example, was challenged personally and professionally when in the mid-seventies Indian children were bussed to the public schools. Respected as a successful teacher, disciplinarian and administrator she now had to confront cultural assimilation of Indian children, knowing only too well from her own childhood the inherent conflict in the meeting of these two cultures. As a nurse, Rebecca did not face the same dilemma. In her own time, she chose to serve on boards of local native organizations on Prince Edward Island and eventually became involved on a national level with the Inuit and Indian nurses' organization. Before Joan died in 1987, she had claimed her Indian status under the membership amendment to the Indian Act of 1985 and was faced with what to do with the rest of her life.

The Sark sons, on the other hand, were destined to return to the Reserve. The oldest boy, Ray, a successful business man in California for over a decade, returned promptly to his Island home after his mother's death and became engrossed in the native culture. His fascination with his roots found expression in a handicraft shop adjacent to his home, featuring a collection of high-quality items made by Indians of different nations. Charles, the youngest son, experienced a more difficult transition. He had left home to complete his schooling as a young adolescent and had lived and worked in a predominantly Irish community for over twenty years. When he returned to Lennox Island in 1974 he had forgotten his native language. Sensitive to his own cultural deprivation, as education director on the Reserve, he is supportive of language instruction and cultural awareness programs in the school and community at large; as representative of the Lennox Island Band on the Minegoo Indian Arts and Crafts Society of Prince Edward Island, he is eager to promote the growth and development of traditional native handicrafts. Jack, on the other hand, always maintained a strong Indian identity. He left the Reserve in the fifties only because it offered him no economic opportunities, he kept close ties with his home. The Micmacs were his people; he belonged to them and he loved them. This he demonstrated when he accepted the position of Band Chief in 1972. A successful entrepreneur, he was elected for the seventh consecutive term in 1989. The record of his accomplishments as Chief constitutes to a large extent the history of the Lennox Island Band of Micmac Indians during the fourth quarter of the 20th century.

After his election as Chief in 1972, to the astonishment of his mother, Jack the philosopher became Jack the doer. That year Reserve programs, which had hitherto been administered by the Departments of Indian Affairs and National Health and Welfare, became the responsibility of the Band government. These included basic services in housing, roads, water, and sewerage; programs in health, education, welfare, recreation, and cultural pursuits; the hiring and training of staff to operate the services and programs. Basic funding for these projects was provided by the two federal departments; extra funding was available for company-orientated projects through the Department of Regional Expansion and for project-oriented programmes through Manpower and Immigration. The young Chief made a point of recruiting competent staff who shared his dream for the future of the Reserve and its people. Once the causeway was a reality, he and his councillors took advantage of every opportunity to advance the living and working conditions of the members of the Lennox Island Band. (The Scotchfort, Morell and Rocky Point reserves were not their responsibility now that they were established as a separate band, the Abegweit Band.)

A new approach to community development had been initiated by the former chief, but those projects unfortunately terminated with his departure from Lennox Island. In 1972 a non-profit company owned by the Band—the Lennox Island Co-operative, later known as Mahemigew Incorporated—was formed and commercial ventures were begun in such resource-related industries as farming, fishing, forestry, and handicrafts. It was felt that income from these industries based on jobs would help reduce the number of welfare recipients. While all these projects were not equally successful, by the end of the Chief's first year in office, a revitalization of Micmac culture had taken place.

Through the Opportunities for Youth (OFY) program, houses were painted, lawns landscaped, flowers and shrubbery planted; the old parochial house was restored and converted to an Indian museum with murals depicting Indian legends and history, cabinets displaying Indian handicrafts, documents, and books; and, an instructor was engaged to teach Micmac language to the children in the school and to the adults in the community. On St. Anne's Day, July 29, 1973, multifarious displays of native talent marked the PEI Centennial Celebrations. The school children, attired in native dress were featured in a pageant depicting the history of the Micmac tribe, after which they sang the Indian National Anthem in Micmac. The craft shop, opened to tourists two weeks prior to the feast day, was selling locally-made handicraft productions in bead, birch, wood, and leather. Displays of Indian handicrafts and demonstrations of basket-weaving were on-going throughout the day. Besides local talent, a fascinating display of Indian dancing was provided by a group of Maliseet Indian Ceremonial Dancers from the Indian reserve at Tobique, New Brunswick.

The Band Council felt strongly that the primary industries of fishing and farming should continue to provide the basis of the Reserve's economy and consistently directed their attention to the development of these areas. In 1973 the oyster fishery was given a boost when a plant was constructed with facilities for the cleaning and grading of oysters. This industry expanded over the years and products were sold to the Maritime Fisherman's Union, to buyers in Montreal and Toronto, and to markets in the United States. As of 1987, the oyster industry has operated as a private enterprise. The latest cooperative venture in fishing is the Lennox Island Fisheries Incorporated. Started in 1989, it is located off the Reserve, at Milligan's wharf, Freeland, and comprises salting, pickling, drying, smoking, marinating, and packaging fresh and frozen products.

The farming of peat moss and blueberries are the fastest growing industries. In 1980 horticultural-grade peat moss was harvested from one of three bogs on the Reserve and transported in bulk to the Gulf Island Peat Company in Foxley River where it was packaged and sold. By 1983 Lennox Island had its own peat processing plant and sold the finished product directly to local, regional, and international markets through Mahemigew Incorporated. Five years later a new peat bog was purchased off the Reserve. Blueberry farming harvested 1600 kilograms in 1983, and most of the crop was sold to Cavendish Farms on Prince Edward Island. The industry expanded quickly and berries are now being shipped to markets in the United States.

Besides projects in aquaculture and agriculture, traditional Micmac arts and crafts are bring revived in co-operation with the Abegweit Band. In 1985 the Minegoo Indian Arts and Crafts Production Centre opened for business in East Royalty featuring 26 types of baskets, including the once famous potato basket. There are long-range plans to include pottery and blankets. Meanwhile, the focus is on training and on the development of the native cottage-craft industry.

An integral part of development has been new communal facilities. A health clinic has been in place since 1973, a new school named for the Chief's father—the John J. Sark Memorial School—was opened in 1981, and a new recreational complex in 1988. Since 1985 the population has doubled and houses have been and are being constructed to accommodate new residents.

The two Micmac bands on Prince Edward Island have finalized a more flexible funding arrangement with the federal government. Although this is interpreted as a step towards self-government, from Chief Jack Sark's perspective, they do not have anything close to the independence enjoyed by the municipal governments on Prince Edward Island.

Under Chief Jack Sark's administration, St. Anne's Day continues to be the major cultural event of the year for the Lennox Island Band of Micmac Indians. Priority is still given to the feast as a religious experience, and the entire Sark family maintain a high profile in the liturgy of the day. Thus, the Sarks have chosen to exercise their leadership roles—whether hereditary or natural—as they read the signs of the times and move forward with their people into the 21st century.

Endnotes

1 The Canadian Visitor

1. Robert H. Davis, "Love Saga of the Red Man," *Canada Cavalcade* (New York: Appleton-Century Co., 1937), 310. See also, St.Dunstan's University, *Centennial Booklet and Registry of All Students Registered since January 17, 1885. Alumni Directory* (Charlottetown: St. Dunstan's Alumni Association, August 2-5, 1954), 65 - 159. The late Mrs. Patricia Saunders of Kensington, Prince Edward Island had in her possession a photo of the football team. Her late husband, Mr. James Saunders, was a classmate of John Sark and was a member of the same football team. A poem featured in the St.Dunstan's College publication *Red and White* pays tribute to the individual players on the football team. The second stanza runs thus: Gillis, Gillis, Sark and Keoughan;/That's the line that guards our back;/But who boots the ball the best of all,/Is the half-back called Sark.

2. *Daily Gleaner*, Fredericton, New Brunswick, December 17, December 21, 1914. The honour roll of the Twenty-fourth Battery was published on December 18, 1914. See also the issues dated February 16, 17, 18, 19, 20, 1915.

3. Davis, "Love Saga of the Red Man," 311.

4. According to John J. Sark's Army Record, he did not leave Shorncliffe until June 1, and he crossed the Channel to France on June 6, 1915.

2 The View from Cliffe Cottage

1. See N. A. Norris, "A Short Account of the History of St. Bernard's Hospital," (mimeographed), n.d., 56.

2. Hanwell Asylum, *Staff Register*, 1875-1914.

3. Hanwell Asylum, Minute Book #58, June 7, 1915, 64. See also *Staff Register June 1, 1877-January 9, 1919*. This so-called Default Book was found with the help of the Librarian in the basement of St. Bernard's Hospital. It includes details of infractions of the rules by the staff, including at least three earlier incidents including Elsie Houghton.

3 "In Sickness and in Health..."

1. Vera Brittain, *Testament to Youth: an Autobiographical Study of the Years 1900-1925* (New York; the Macmillan Co., 1934).

2. Davis, "Love Saga of the Red Man," 311-12.

3. This might have been the beautiful Beachborough Place, Shorncliffe, which Lady Markham gave to the military for a hospital.

ENDNOTES

4. See *Guardian* (Charlottetown), December 24, 1914, 4. Buckingham Palace Riding School, "Programme of Entertainment to Wounded Soldiers and Sailors," March 22, 1916. The complete programme, including the words of music for the songs, is in the possession of his youngest son Charlie, Lennox Island.

5. The letter to Father John A. McDonald from Travers Buxton is dated May 9, 1916.

6. Marion Gridley, *The Story of Pocahontas* (Chicago: Rand McNally and Co., 1942).

7. Interview with Eleanor Callow, Charlottetown, June 26, 1988.

8. *Daily Gleaner*, March 8, 1915.

9. Hanwell, Minute Book #59, December 4 and 18, 1916. Elsie's resignation was accepted by the Committee on December 4; she left on December 9. According to the notation her conduct was satisfactory!

10. Hanwell, Minute Book #61, April 8, 1918.

4 Journey to the Island

1. Charles Dalton, pioneer in the black and silver fox farming industry was born in Tignish, Prince Edward Island, on June 9, 1850. He represented Prince County in the local legislature from 1912-1919 and was appointed Lieutenant-Governor in 1930. He died in 1933 before his term expired. In 1917 His holiness Pope Benedict XV conferred on him the title of Knight Commander of the order of St. Gregory the Great. As a member of the first association to become involved in the campaign against tuberculosis, the Anti-Tuberculosis Society (1888-1919), he learned of the prevalence of T.B. on "the Island" and donated $53,000 to buy a site in North Wiltshire where he would supply the funds to build and furnish a twenty-four patient capacity sanatorium.

2. F.H. MacArthur, "Minegoo Was Made in Heaven," in *Legends of Prince Edward Island* (Charlottetown, PEI: H.M. Simpsons, Ltd., 1966), 8-10: see also, Errol Sharpe, *A People's History of Prince Edward Island* (Toronto: Steel Rail Publishing, 1976), 4.

3. PA PEI, Taped interview of Mrs. John Sark by Mrs. Helen MacDonald for CBC Radio, June 1961.

5 Elsie's Island Home

1. Interview with Reverend Bennet Macdonald, Charlottetown, P.E.I., August 22, 1985.

2. See taped interview of Mrs. John Sark, June 1961, and letter to the Indian Commissioner in Ottawa from Ex-Chief John Sark, October 9, 1928.

3. Gwen Newcombe heard of this detail from her mother, Mrs. Gardiner Newcombe, Port Hill.

4. Calvin Martin, "The European Impact on the Culture of a Northeastern Algonquin Tribe: an Ecological Interpretation," *The William and Mary Quarterly XXXI* (January 1974), 25-26.

5. Marie Battiste, "The Micmac Indians," Lecture delivered at Dalhousie University, Faculty of Education, Halifax, Nova Scotia, July 18, 1989. See also

Marie Ann Battiste, "An Historical Investigation of the Social and Cultural Consequences of Micmac Literacy," (D. Ed. Thesis, Stanford University, 1984), 115.

6. J. Henri Blanchard, *Acadiens de l'Île-du-Prince-Edouard* (L'imprimerie acadienne Ltée, 1956), 7.

7. Leslie F. S. Upton, *Micmacs and Colonists: Indian-White Relations in the Maritimes, 1713-1867 (Vancouver: University of British Columbia Press, 1979)*, 113.

8. Upton, *Micmacs and Colonists*, 120; "Indians and Islanders," 38.

9. James Wilson, *Canada's Indians, Minority Rights, Report #21* (First published in 1974. New edition, London: March, 1977), 20.

10. The text of "Micmac Talk" is in the possession of his son Charles H. who was named executor of his mother's will.

6 The Lennox Island Reserve: 1918

1. General informtion on the status quo of the Reserve in 1918 was derived from interviews with the local people living in the region at the time.

2. Most of the statistical data used in this chapter are taken from the Indian Affairs reports for the years 1918 and 1919 and, therefore, provide as accurate a picture as possible of the actual state of the Reserve at the time of Elsie's arrival. For census information, see "Report of the Deputy General of Indian Affairs for the Year Ended March 31, 1918," 9 George V, Sessional Paper #27A, p56; 58; and 10 George V, #27A, 1920, 7.

3. John A. McDonald, "Report to the Department of Indian Affairs," 6 George V, A., 1916, 126.

4. John A. McDonald, "Report of the Superintendent for the Province, 1914," 115-6.

5. "Dame Louisa Augusta Wood," in *Wills and Administration, Vol 12, 1872*, Somerset House, London, England. The Will was signed on May 5, 1870. NA, Department of Indian Affairs, "Lennox Island Reserve," C-11,108 #2307. A copy of the Deed of Lennox Island is dated June 2, 1870. On January 19, 1911, J.D. McLean, Assistant Deputy and Secretary to the Department of Indian Affiars wrote to John E. Campbell, Registrar of Deeds, Summerside, P.E.I., requesting whether the deed to Lennox Island was still registered in the name of the trustees of the Aborigines Protection Society. His response, dated January 13, 1911, confirmed that it was. The department then took the necessary steps to have the title of the property vested in His Majesty the King as represented by the Superintendent General of Indian Affairs for the Indians of Prince Edward Island. Following the advice of the society, this was legally effected on May 30, 1912, by order of the Court of Chancery. See also 5 George V, ca12.

6. According to Elsie in her 1961 taped interview, there were only three women on the Reserve in 1918 who could speak English.

7 Convalescent on the Reserve

1. Telephone interview with Mrs. George Clow, Bedeque, Prince Edward Island, 1986.

2. Information about the St. Anne's Day celebration was derived from newspaper accounts and interviews with the oldest residents in the area.

3. Annual Report to the Department of Indian Affairs, 1919, 10 George V, A., 1920, 18.

8 Volunteer Community-Worker

1. Taped interview of Mrs. John Sark, CBC Radio, June, 1961.
2. Father Pacifique Buisson, a Capuchin priest, came to Canada from France in 1894 and was missionary to the Micmacs from 1901 until 1934. It was he who revived the religious rituals and traditions which had been earlier established by Father Pierre Antoine Maillard. For further information, see Marie Ann Battiste, "An Historical Investigation of the Social and Cultural Consequences of Micmac Literacy," D. Ed. Dissertation, Stanford University, 1983, 136-138.
3. John Lenhart, OM, cap. *History of Micmac Ideographic Manual.* History relating to Manual of Prayers, Instructions, Psalms and Hymns used by Micmac Indians of Eastern Canada and Newfoundland (Pittsburgh, PA: the Nova Scotia Native Communications Society, 1932).

9 The Politics of Mistrust

1. Interview with Mrs. Harold Brown, Grand River, P.E.I., September 17, 1982.
2. Interview with Mrs. Robert Strongman, St. Eleanor's, P.E.I., August 2, 1985.
3. Interview with Mrs. Hatfield Maynard, Tyne Valley, P.E.I., August 6, 1985.
4. Interview with Mrs. Carmen MacNeil, Tyne Valley, P.E.I., August 6, 1985.
5. Interview with Mrs. Howard MacKinnon, Grand River, P.E.I., August 11, 1987.
6. NA, Lennox Island, "Elections of Chiefs and Councillors, 1897-1935," in NA RG10, Vol. 7936, File 32057, Pt I, Reel C-13508.
7. For all correspondence on this subject herein: NA, Lennox Island, "Teachers-General Administration, 1894-1938." RG10, Vol. 6059, File 270-1, Pt.1, Reel# C68162.

10 Witness to Survival

1. Interview with Mrs. Joan (Sark) Beaudin, Chatham, New Brunswick, July 25, 1986.
2. Interview with Sister Martha, September 26, 1987.
3. Sister Florence McTague, "A Love Story: the War Bride from the White Cliffs of Dover," P.E.I. Heritage Foundation (mimeographed), November 9, 1978, 3.
4. Interview with Sister Rebecca, September 26, 1987.
5. Interview with Mrs. Sarah Tuplin, August 22, 1985.
6. Interview with Reverend Bennet Macdonald, August 20, 1984.
7. The award, testimonial and a handwritten copy of the tribute are in the possession of the Sark family. See also, *The Guardian* (Charlottetown), July 31, 1935, 9; and, August 7, 1935, 10.
8. NA, Indian Affairs, RG10, Vol. 6059, File 210-1, C-8162, Part I, Lennox Island, P.E.I., December 27 (CP), (1935). (Probably from the Summerside Journal.)

9. Telephone interview with Mrs. Lou Roper, Southport, September 21, 1985. Later Mrs. Roper shared with the writer a number of pictures taken of the children at Lennox Island.

10. Following correspondence in this chapter can be referenced as follows: NA, Indian Affairs, RG10, Vol. 6059, File 270-1, Part II. "Prince Edward Island, Lennox Island School, Teachers...1938-1948," July 11, 1938.

11 The Price of Love

1. Davis, "Love Saga of the Red Man."

2. Interview with Mrs. Alice Sharpe, Ellerslie, August 6, 1985. She was also a WWI bride from Birmingham, England, whose husband spoke very highly of John Sark. She was eager to learn more about the fantastic Mrs. Sark she had heard so much about, so when the Indians came to her door peddling wares she inquired: "What is Mrs. Sark like?" Their response "Just a squaw like any other!"

3. Interview with Sister Mary Henry Mulligan, CSM, Charlottetown, October 24, 1987. See also *The Guardian* (Charlottetown), September 6, 1936, 6.

4. Davis, "Love Saga of the Red Man," 313.

5. Interview with Mrs. Jessie Brown, Grand River, September 17, 1982. 14. Prince Edward Island School Report for the year ending June 30, 1943, 6

6. William Arthur Reddin, *My Canoe and I*, (Charlottetown, P.E.I., n.d.) 30-31.

7. Interview with Sister Mary Henry Mulligan, October 24, 1987.

8. Interview with Sarah (Mitchell) Tuplin, Lower Montague, August 29, 1984.

12 New Beginnings

1. Interview with Mrs. Doris Murphy, Locke Shore, July 29, 1986.

2. Taped interview with Mrs. John Sark by Mrs. Helen MacDonald for CBC Radio, June 1961.

3. Interview with Mrs. Marguerite Maynard., Tyne Valley, August 6, 1985.

13 A Decision to Stay

1. Sister Mary Immaculate Loughran, "Compilation of a Brief History of Lennox Island" (Mimeographed booklet, n.d.) 8.

2. Interview with Sister Mary Magdalen Connolly, July 29, 1983.

3. Interview with Ellen Taylor, Southampton, July 24, 1984.

4. Interview with Mrs. Eleanor Callow, Charlottetown, June 22, 1988.

5. Sister Mary Immaculate, "Compilation of a Brief History of Lennox Island" (Mimeographed, n.d.) 20-21. Among participants in the plays still living on Prince Edward Island are Ray Sark and Joe LaBobe from Lennox Island; Bertha Francis from Rocky Point.

6. Interview with Mr. Joseph Tuplin, Lower Montague, September 28, 1982.

7. Interview with Mrs. Joan Beaudin, August 5, 1986.

8. Interview with Sister Mary Immaculate, Charlottetown, August 22, 1985.

14 Losses and Gains

1. H. M. Jones, Indian Affairs Branch, Department of Citizenship and Immigration, *Annual Report, 1960-1961,* 25

2. Interview with Eleanor Callow, Charlottetown, June 22, 1988.

3. Interview with Mrs. Alfred Hennessey, Charlottetown, October 12, 1982.

4. Frederic J. Gross, "Preparing for a Future: a Study of the Micmac Indians of the Lennox Island Reserve," Final Report, Department of Sociology and Anthropology, Saint Dunstan's University, July 1969, viii.

5. Interview with Chief James Sark, Rocky Point, September 1, 1988.

6. Text of sermon preached at the funeral Mass for Rev. Emmet W. M. MacInnis, April 6, 1967. Courtesy of Mrs. Joseph MacInnis, Charlottetown.

15 Resignation to God's Will

1. Canada, Department of Regional Economic Expansion, *Federal-Provincial Agreement Covering a Comprehensive Development Plan for Prince Edward Island* (Ottawa: Queen's Printer, 1969).

2. Harold Cardinal, *The Unjust Society: the Tragedy of Canada's Indians* (Edmonton: Hurtig Publishers, 1969)

3. Interview with Chief James Sark, Rocky Point, September 1, 1988.

4. Interview with Mrs. Angie Mathers, Rocky Point, July 28, 1983.

5. Interview with Sister Christine Doyle, Saint Theresa's, Septmber 30, 1982.

6. The story is contained in the local newspapers from November 22, 1971 through November 26, 1971: *The Journal-Pioneer,* (Summerside) November 24, 16, 19, 1971; *The Guardian* (Charlottetown), November 22, 1971.

7. *The Journal-Pioneer* (Summerside), April 17, 1973, 3; May 10, 1973, 5; *The Guardian* (Charlottetown), 5.

Bibliography

Government Records

British Museum, London. Map of Dover. Heliozincographed from 2300 Plans and Published by the Director General of the Ordinance Survey Office, Southampton. Surveyed in 1858-62. Revised in 1906. Third edition, 1908. June 5, 1909.

Greater London Record Office and Library. London County Asylum: Hanwell, Sub-Committee Minute Books 1913-1918.

_____. Hanwell Asylum: Staff Register. Vol I, January 6, 1877-September 1, 1919.

_____. Hanwell Asylum: Staff Register of Officers and Servants, 1875-1914.

_____. Hanwell Asylum: Staff Register. "Non-Established Nurses, May 25, 1912-July 26, 1914."

Prince Edward Island Collection, University of Prince Edward Island. "An Act Relating to the Indians of Prince Edward Island, April 14, 1856."

Public Archives, Nova Scotia. Intercolonial Railway of Canada. General Passenger Timetable, 1890, 1912. RG28, Vol. 63, #30 and 31.

National Archives of Canada. Government Records. Personnel Records Office File. Military Records of Charles J. Houghton, Henry W. Houghton and Jack R. Houghton; John J. Sark.

_____. Halifax Passenger Lists. SS OLYMPIC, Transport #2810, 20-3-1918. Reel T-4757.

_____. Indian Affairs. Lennox Island Reserve. Purchase of Lennox Island by the Aborigines Protection Society for the Use and Benefit of the Indians. 1874-1912. Red Series, RG10 Volume 1907 File 2307, Part 0, C-11,108.

_____. Indian Affairs Central Registry. Indian Soldier Settlement, 1919-1942. RG10 Volume 7523 File 25,057-3, Part 0, C-14802.

_____. Indian Affairs, Elections. Prince Edward Island, Lennox Island. Elections of Chiefs and Councillors 1897-1935. RG10 Volume 7936 File 32-57, Part 1, C-13, 508.

_____. Indian Affairs, School Files. Prince Edward Island—Lennox Island School—Teachers—General Administration. 1894-1938. RG10, Volume 6059 File 270-1, Part 1, C-8162.

_____. Prince Edward Island—Lennox Island School—Teachers—General Administration—Map—1938-1948. RG10 Volume 6059 File 270-1, Part 2, C-8162.

_____. Prince Edward Island—Lennox Island School—Salaries. 1912-1934, 1945. RG10 Volume 6059 File 270-3, Part 1, C-8162.

_____. Prince Edward Island—Lennox Island School—Building Maintenance—Supplies—Accounts—General Administration. 1869-1875, 1888-1899. RG10 Volume 6059 File 270-5, Part 1, C-8162.

_____. Prince Edward Island—Lennox Island School—Building Maintenance—Supplies—Accounts. 1918-1938. RG10 Volume 6059 file 270-5, Part 2, C-8162.

_____. Prince Edward Island—Lennox Island School—Establishment—Building Maintenance—Supplies—Accounts. 1946-1949. RG10 Volume 6059 File 270-5, Part 3, C-8162.

_____. Prince Edward Island—Lennox Island School—Building Maintenance—Supplies—Accounts. 1948-1949. RG Volume 6059 File 270-5, Part 4, C-8162.

Public Archives, Prince Edward Island. Dalton Sanatorium Commission. Letterbook, 1913-1916. Acc. 2541.

_____. Anti-tuberculosis Society Minutes, Charlottetown Branch, 1909-1925. Acc. 3414.

_____. Taped Interview of Mrs. John Sark, CFCY Radio Program, 1961. Interviewed by Helen MacDonald.

Public Record Office, London. British Military Records, Royal Artillery. W097 3093 Charles Fisher Houghton; W097 5162 Charles James Houghton.

_____. Index Regimental Registers, 1761-1924. Army Births and Baptisms (AB91), Vol. 1470.

_____. General Index of Births, Marriages and Deaths Recorded in England and Wales since July 1, 1837. General Register Office, St. Catherine's House.

_____. Wills and Administration. Vol. 12, 1872. Somerset House.

Government Publications

Canada. Department of Indian Affairs. *Annual Reports. 1864-1974.* Secretary of State, 1868-1873; Department of the Interior, 1874-1879; Department of Indian Affairs, 1880-1933; Department of Mines & Resources, Indian Affairs Branch, 1934-1949; Department of Citizenship & Immigration, Indian Affairs Branch, 1950-1965; Department of Indian Affairs & Northern Development, 1966-1974.

Canada. Department of Indian Affairs and Northern Development. *A Survey of the Contemporary Indians of Canada.* 1966 Vol I; 1967 Vol II. Edited by H.B. Hawthorne.

_____. *Indians of Quebec and the Maritime Provinces.* Ottawa, 1971.

_____. *The Canadian Indian, Quebec and the Atlantic Provinces.* Ottawa, 1973.

Canada. Department of Energy, Mines and Resources, Surveys and Mapping Branch. *Geographical Names of Prince Edward Island.* Toponymy Study 1 by Alan Rayburn, 1953.

Canada. House of Commons. *Debates,* 1916-1918.

_____. *Indian Self-Government in Canada. Report of the Special Committee.* Chairman Mr. Keith Palmer, Issue No. 40, October 12, 1983; October 20, 1983.

_____. *Sessional Papers,* 1867-1925.

_____. Secretary of State. *Speaking Together: Canada's Native Women*. Ottawa, 1975.

Canada. Department of Regional Economic Expansion. *Federal-Provincial Agreement Covering a Comprehensive Development Plan for Prince Edward Island*. Ottawa, 1969.

Canadian Archives. *Documents Relating to the Constitutional History of Canada, 1759-1791*. Selected and edited with notes by Adam Shortt and Arthur G. Doughty. Ottawa: S.E. Dawson, 1907.

National Museum of Canada. *Historical Background of the Micmac Indians of Canada*, by Wilson D. Wallis. Bulletin 173 (1959), 42-63.

_____. *Indians of Canada*, by Diamond Jeness. Bulletin 65 (1960).

_____. *The Micmac Indians of Restigouche; History and Contemporary Description* by Philip K. Bock. Bulletin 213 (1966).

_____. *Approaches to Native History in Canada*. Conference held at the National Museum of Man, October 1975. Edited by D.A. Muise.

_____. *The Changing Economic Roles for Micmac Men and Women: an Ethnohistorical Analysis* by Ellice Becker Gonzalez. Ottawa, 1981.

Prince Edward Island. Journals of the Legislative Assembly. *Annual Reports of Indian Commissioners, 1857-1872*.

_____. *Revised statutes of Prince Edward Island, 1862*.

Books

Brittain, Vera. *Testament of Youth: An Autobiographical Study of the Years 1900-1925*. New York: The Macmillan Co., 1934.

Brown, R. Allen. *Ancient Monuments and Historic Buildings: Dover Castle*. Department of Environment. Swindon: Her Majesty's Stationery Office, Swindon Press, Ltd., 1967.

Buckingham, Christopher. *Catholic Dover. A Book to Celebrate the Centennial Anniversary of St. Paul's Church*. Lydden, Dover, Kent: Thomas Becket Books, 1968.

Campbell, Duncan. *History of Prince Edward Island*. Charlottetown: Bremner Brothers, 1875.

Cardinal, Harold. *The Unjust Society: The Tragedy of Canada's Indians*. Edmonton: Hurtig Publishers Ltd., 1969.

Davis, Robert H. *Canada Cavalcade: The Maple Leaf Dominion from Atlantic to Pacific*. New York: D. Appleton-Century Co., Inc., 1937.

Gordon, Lawrence L. *British Battles and Medals*. Aldershot: Gale and Polden Ltd., 1962.

Gould, Gary P. and Allan J. Semple. *Our Land: the Maritimes; the Basis of the Indian Claims in the Maritime Provinces of Canada*. Fredericton, N.B.: St. Anne's Print Press, 1980.

Gridley, Marion. *The Story of Pocahontas*. Chicago: Rand McNally & Co., 1942.

Harvey, D.C. *The French Régime in PEI*. New Haven: Yale Press, 1926.

Hamilton, W.D. *The Federal Indian Day Schools of the Maritimes*. Micmac-Malisset Institute, 1986.

BIBLIOGRAPHY

Hopkins, J. Castell. *The Canadian Annual Review of Public Affairs*. Toronto: The Annual Review Publishing Co., 1911.

Hymns, Ancient and Modern for Use in the Services of the Church. Complete edition. London: William Lowes and Sons, n.d.

Intercolonial Railway, Prince Edward Island Railway. *Summer Provinces by the Sea*. n.d.

Lenhart, John, O.M., Cap. *History of Micmac Ideographic Manual*. History Relating to Manual of Prayers, Instructions, Psalms and Hymns in Micmac Ideograms used by Micmac Indians of Eastern Canada and Newfoundland. Pittsburg, PA. The Nova Scotia Native Communications Society, 1932.

MacArthur, F.H. *Legends of Prince Edward Island*. Charlottetown: H.M. Simpson, Ltd., 1966; 6th ed., 1974.

Macmillan, John C. *The Early History of the Catholic Church in Prince Edward Island, 1721-1835*. Quebec: l'Evenement Printing Co., 1905.

_____. *The History of the Catholic Church in Prince Edward Island from 1835 till 1891*. Quebec: l'Evenement Printing Co., 1913.

MacMillan, Cyrus. *Glooskap's Country and Other Indian Tales*. Toronto: Oxford University Press, 1955.

Manchester, William. *The Last Lion: Winston Spencer Churchill. Visions of Glory 1874-1932*. Little, Brown and Company, 1983.

Mee, Arthur. *The King's England: Kent. A Unique Guide to 10,000 Towns and Villages of England as History Has Made Them*. Fully revised and edited by C.R. Councer. Hodder and Stoughton, 1969.

Miller, Alice Duer. *The White Cliffs*. New York: Coward-McCann, Inc., 1940.

Padovano, Anthony T. *Belief in Human Life*. New Jersey: Pastoral Educational Services, 1960.

Reddin, William Arthur. *Canoe and I: Around the Island in a Canoe*. Charlottetown, PEI: Private Printing, n.d.

R.L.O. and Others. *War-Time Verses*. Dundee: James P. Mathew and Co., 1918.

Sharpe, Errol. *A People's History of Prince Edward Island*. Toronto: Steel Rail Publishing, 1976.

Stevens, G.R. *Canadian National Railways: Towards the Inevitable, 1892-1922*, Vol. 2. Toronto: Clarke, Irwin and Co., Ltd., 1966.

The Holy Bible. King James Version, Red Letter edition. New York: The World Publishing Co., n.d.

The Island Minstrel: a Collection of the Poetical Writings of John Le Page. Charlottetown, P.E.I.: George T. Haszard, Printers, 1860.

The Weekday Missal. Glasgow: William Collins Sons & Co., 1975.

Treasure, G.R.R. *Who's Who in History: England 1789-1837*. Oxford: Basil Blackwell, 1974.

Upton, Leslie F.S. *Micmacs and Colonists: Indian - White Relations in the Maritimes 1713-1867*. Vancouver: University of British Columbia Press, 1979.

Wallis, Wilson D. and Ruth Sawtell Wallis. *The Micmac Indians of Eastern Canada*. Minneapolis: University of Minnesota Press, 1955.

Welby, Doug. *The Tidy Ruin. History of the Parish Church of St. James the Apostle, Dover*. Published on behalf of the Dover Archeological Group, 1976.

"X". *War Poems*. London: Martin Secker, 1916.

Zonta Club of Charlottetown. *Outstanding Women of Prince Edward Island*. Summerside: William and Crue Ltd., 1981.

Articles

"At Charlottetown, P.E.I., Canada Greets Her King," *Macleans* May 15, 1939, p. 70.

Battiste, Marie. "An Historical Investigation of the Social and Cultural Consequences of Micmac Literacy." D. Ed. Dissertation, Stanford University, 1983.

Blair, Donald. "From Old Restraints to Modern Freedom at Historic St. Bernard's Hospital," *Proceedings of the Third World Congress of Psychiatry*. Montreal: McGill University. Press, 1961, Vol II.

"Breaking a Chief's Iron Rule," Provincial Report, Prince Edward Island. *Atlantic Insight*, August 1986, p. 7.

Chamberlain, Alexander F. "Indians of the Eastern Provinces of Canada." *Report of the Minister of Education Archaeological Report, Ontario, 1905*. Toronto, 1906. pp. 122-136.

Daniel, A.W. "Brief History of Hanwell Mental Hospital, July 1831-July 1941." Mimeographed, St. Bernard's Hospital Library, n.d.

Elvins, S.W.G. "Invicta": the Story of a Royal Castle. Dover: Giraud, pamphlet, n.d.

"Fancy Fair at Hanwell Lunatic Asylum." *Illustrated London News*, May 20, 1848.

Fitzherbert, Katrin. "Monument to Humanity: Hanwell Lunatic Asylum," *Country Life*, May 22, 1986, pp. 1460-1461.

Gill, Helen M. "The Great White Plague: Tuberculosis, and the Evolution of Government Responsibility for Public Health on P.E.I., 1881-1931." Unpublished History Honours Programme Thesis. University of Prince Edward Island, December, 1984.

Gross, Frederic J. "Preparing for a Future: A Study of the Micmac Indians of Lennox Island Reserve," *Report to the Indian Affairs Branch, Department of Indian Affairs and Northern Development and St. Dunstan's University*. Charlottetown, St. Dunstan's University, 1969.

Lafferty, J.F. "Prince Edward Island Railway," *Canadian National Magazine*, May 1951, pp. 9-11.

Loughran, Sister Mary Immaculata. "Compilation of Brief History of Lennox Island." Charlottetown: Mimeographed Booklet [1983].

Maloney, John. "And in the Beginning," in *Canada's Smallest Province: a History of Prince Edward Island*. F.W.P. Bolger (ed.) Charlottetown, P.E.I., Centennial Commission, 1973.

Martin, Calvin. "The European impact on culture of a north-eastern Algonquian tribe: an ecological interpretation," *William and Mary Quarterly*, XXXI, (January, 1974), 3-26.

McQuaig, Katherine. "From School Reform to Social Science: the Changing Role of Volunteers in the Anti-Tuberculosis Campaign, 1900-1930." *Canadian Historical Review*. LXI (1980), p. 481.

McTague, Sister Florence. "A Love Story: the War Bride from the White Cliffs of Dover," PEI Heritage Foundation, November 7, 1978 (mimographed).

Norris, H.A. "A Short Account of the History of St. Bernard's Hospital." London Borough of Ealing Public Library, Mimeographed, n.d., 11 pp. _____. "The Hanwell Asylum, St. Bernard's Hospital: a Short Historical Account by a Former Chaplain of the Hospital," Greater London Record Office and History Library, Mimeographed, 71 pp. [1986].

Pollard, J. B. "Historical Sketch of the Eastern Region of New France and Prince Edward Island: Military and Civil, 1898."

"The New Telephone Line Between Prince Edward Island and New Brunswick," MT & T Monthly Bulletin, September 15, 1918, p. 109.

Upton, L.F.S. "Colonists and Micmacs." Journal of Canadian Studies. X (August, 1975). 44-56.

_____. "Indians and Islanders, the Micmacs of Colonial PEI." Acadiensis (Autumn, 1976). 21-42.

Wallis, Wilson D. and Wallis, Ruth Sawtell. "Culture Loss and Culture Change among the Micmacs of the Canadian Maritime Provinces, 1912-1950." Kroeber Anthropological Society Papers, VIII (1953), 100-129.

Wilson, James. "Canada's Indians." Minority Rights Group, Report #21, First published, 1974. New Edition, London, March 1977.

Weale. "The Middlesex County Lunatic Asylum, Hanwell." New Survey of London, II (1853), 601-607.

Miscellaneous Records

Atlas of the Province of PEI and the World. Toronto: Cummins Map Co., n.d.

Gooding, M. "London Borough of Ealing: Historical Notes, 1975," Ealing Public Library, London, England.

"Grand Shaft," Schools Information Sheet, Dover Museum, Dover, England, n.d.

Illustrated Historical Atlas of the Province of Prince Edward Island, from surveys made under the direction of C.R. Allen, C.E. J.H. Meacham & Co., Pub., 1880. Edited by Mika Pub. Co., Belleville, Ontario, 1977.

Lennox Island Band Council. Brief to the Land Use Commission, 1874.

_____. "Community Profile, Lennox Island, P.E.I." Prepared by Darlene Bernard, October 1982.

_____. "The Micmac People of Lennox Island: a Learning Kit." Prepared by Doreen Sark, Charlottetown: Queen's Printer, 1973.

Milford, C. Map of Prince Edward Island. Charlottetown: G. Ballingall, 1920.

Miscouche Convent, Miscouche, P.E.I. Register of Boarders, 1932-1943.

Our Lady and St. Joseph Church, Hanwell, London, England. Register of Baptisms, 1916.

Our Lady Help of Christians and St. Aloysius Church, Folkestone, Kent, England. Register of Marriages, 1916.

Our Lady of Fatima Convent, Lennox Island, P.E.I. Annals 1958-61; 1968-71.

Prince Edward Island Board of Education. Public School License, 1909. #4068.

Pike's Dover and District Blue Book. Local Directory. The "G.M.F." Blue Book. Originally published by Robinson, Son & Pike; Brighton: Garnett, Mepham and Fisher, Ltd., 1895-1921.

Prince of Wales College and Normal School, Charlottetown, P.E.I. *Annual Reports 1939-1944.*

Roadmasters Registry Book. *Births and Deaths, Lennox Island, 1919-1945.*

Ruth Benedict Papers, "Adventures in Womanhood," unpublished manuscript, Vassar College, Poughkeepsie, N.Y. Quoted in Joyce Antler, "Feminism As Life Process," *Feminist Studies 7*, I (Spring, 1981).

St. Agnes Church, Debec, Carleton Co., New Brunswick. *Register of Baptisms, 1888.*

St. Anne's Church, Lennox Island, PEI. *Records of Baptism, Marriages and Deaths 1812-1987.*

St. Dunstan's Basilica, Charlottetown, PEI. *Register of Baptisms.*

St. Dunstan's University. *Centennial Booklet and Registry of All Students Registered since January 17, 1885. Alumni Directory.* pp. 65-159. St. Dunstan's Alumni Association, August 2-5, 1954.

St. Mary's Church, Indian River, P.E.I. *Register of Baptisms.*

Shubenacadie Residential School. *Annals, January 27, 1930- June 24, 1967.*

The *"Standard" Directory of Dover and Neighbouring Villages.* Kent, England. Dover: "Standard" Office 1914-1918.

Newspapers

Chronicle-Herald. (Halifax, Nova Scotia) July 3, 1984.

Daily Gleaner. (Fredericton, New Brunswick) 1914-1918.

The Guardian. (Charlottetown, Prince Edward Island) 1917-1987.

The Islander. (Charlottetown, Prince Edward Island) September 29, 1865; September 3, 1869.

The Island Patriot. (Charlottetown, Prince Edward Island) 1915.

Journal/The Pioneer. (Summerside, Prince Edward Island) June 28, 1887-1987.

Index